# THE AMAZING
# SUMMER OF '55

# THE AMAZING SUMMER OF '55

*The year of motor racing's biggest dramas,*
*worst tragedies and greatest victories*

## EOIN YOUNG

*Foreword by Tony Brooks*

**Haynes Publishing**

First published in April 2005

A catalogue record for this book is
available from the British Library

ISBN 1 84425 114 4

Library of Congress catalog card no. 2004 117161

Published by Haynes Publishing, Sparkford,
Yeovil, Somerset BA22 7JJ, UK
Tel: 01963 442030 Fax: 01963 440001
Int. tel: +44 1963 442030 Int. fax: +44 1963 440001
E-mail: sales@haynes.co.uk
Website: www.haynes.co.uk

Haynes North America Inc.,
861 Lawrence Drive, Newbury Park,
California 91320, USA

Designed and typeset by G&M Designs Limited,
Raunds, Northamptonshire

Printed and bound in Britain by
J. H. Haynes & Co. Ltd, Sparkford

Dedication

In appreciation of the huge help from true friends,
saving me from myself and TFW ...

Thank you most sincerely.

# CONTENTS

*Acknowledgements*                                          11
*Foreword*                                                  17
*Introduction*                                              21

1   **January**
    Prince 'Bira' wins in New Zealand              27

2   **January**
    Those searing South American races            33

3   **10 April**
    The saga of Ruth Ellis and David Blakeley     39

4   **1–2 May**
    Moss and the Mille Miglia –
    1,000 miles at 100mph!                        45

5   **May**
    Ferrari's mystery twin-cylinder
    Grand Prix engine                             59

6   **22 May**
In the drink – the tale of the 1955
Monaco Grand Prix!    63

*Plate section*    65–80

7   **25 May**
World Champion Alberto Ascari killed    88

8   **30 May**
Fatal hat-trick at Indy    94

9   **Summer**
Grand Prix du Roc    103

10   **5 June**
Lancia's Spa swansong    111

11   **Summer**
Lancia flatters to demise    116

12   **11–12 June**
New British cars at Le Mans    124

13   **11–12 June**
Disaster at Le Mans    132

14   **June**
The air-brake controversy    160

15   **19 June**
Back to business: Racing goes on in Holland    164

16   **16 July**
     Briton wins the British Grand Prix          168

     *Plate section*                        177–192

17   **7 August**
     Swedish mixture as before                   194

18   **11 September**
     Banking on Monza                            198

19   **17 September**
     Sunshine and shadow at Dundrod              206

20   **30 September**
     James Dean: "Too fast to live,
     too young to die"                           215

21   **8 October**
     First Grand Prix for Cooper in
     "The Car that Jack Built"                   225

22   **16 October**
     Final laurels in Sicily                     230

23   **23 October**
     Tony Brooks wins in Syracuse                236

24   **Epilogue**
     The 300SLR Coupé: A racer that never raced  245

     *Index*                                     251

# ACKNOWLEDGEMENTS

This book has been for me a hugely enjoyable visit to a season of motor sport half a century ago, when the world was very different, a summer when the world of motor sport was changed violently and safety was being mentioned – or at least noticed – seemingly for the first time. It clashed with the sentiments of Earl Howe, then President of the British Racing Drivers' Club, who addressed the drivers on the grid before a British Grand Prix in the late 1940s, saying "Gentlemen, motor racing is dangerous ... and it is up to us to keep it that way!"

It was also a summer when it was good to be British, when that dashingly youthful sportsman Stirling Moss was winning his first Grand Prix – and his home Grand Prix at that – and he amazed Italy and the world by winning the Mille Miglia at record speed in the works Mercedes.

Tony Brooks, the quiet dental student, drove into the history books when he became the first British driver since Henry Segrave, in the 1920s, to win a Grand Prix on a foreign circuit with a British car by dominating the Syracuse Grand Prix in a Connaught, to the total devastation and amazement of the famous and all-conquering Maserati team.

I would like to thank those contemporary writers and sources I have used as research, since 1955 was six seasons before I found myself in Europe and travelling around circuits I had only read about in awe as a young bank clerk in New Zealand. Thanks to Haymarket Publications for the material I borrowed from the race reports in *The Autocar* and *Motor Sport* and I hope that I have used this as a means of honouring my predecessors at the typewriter in those days before laptops. My thanks for the use of the wonderful words by Peter Garnier, who did so much to capture the spirit of racing in that summer of 'fifty-five. It was Peter, then Sports Editor, who invited me to write a page on racing every week in *The Autocar* "because I knew the younger drivers better than he did" in the mid-sixties. I wrote that page for over 30 years.

Thanks to Chris Nixon for his volumes on the cars and drivers in that pivotal season of 1955 when Mercedes and Lancia were at loggerheads and thanks also to Peter Miller who was something of a soldier of writing fortune in the 1950s, covering the races, working with Aston Martin, mates with the drivers and writing books like *The Fast Ones*, much as I did in the 1960s and 1970s when I covered the races and for a time worked with John Wyer's Gulf team, a generation after Miller had worked with him at Aston Martin.

My thanks to Nigel Roebuck, the top motor racing columnist on *Autosport*, who has been a life-long enthusiast, a writer with a sentimental love of the history of the sport and the tenacity to stay involved into the modern era when racing has changed from an exciting amateur sport to a professional arm of show business, fuelled by huge helpings of commercial sponsorship. It was Roebuck's words that he allowed me to use from his interview with Sir Peter Ustinov and his memories of making the classic comedy offering of *The Grand Prix du Roc*, commissioned by a Californian record company in 1955.

Thanks to Mark Hughes at Haynes Publishing for the offer of the idea and the suggestion that I was the person to write this book. Peter Renn has been my right-hand man back at my office base in Bookham, Surrey, and it has been thanks to the ARFS (Amazing Renn Filing System) that I have been able to research from afar. Closer to my laptop while I was finishing the book in Christchurch, New Zealand, has been Milan Fistonic who not only enjoys his impressive library of motor-sporting books, but also knows where all the facts I need are, and can e-mail instant answers to my many queries. Thanks to Milan and to Peter for making sure that I stay with the play.

Thanks to Tony Brooks for his Foreword, a driver I never saw race but who has been warm and entertaining company when he has joined us for lunch at the Barley Mow, a true gentleman and a former Ferrari team driver from an era so different from the modern Michael Schumacher days that it belies comparison.

In fact the comparison is direct between 1955 and 2005. Sex seemed to be safe then and motor racing was danger-ous. Now the reverse rules life and motorsport. In 1955 the drivers were sportsmen who regarded the danger as a necessary aspect, the challenge of the bullfighter, the jousting on the edge with the winner taking all. Now motor racing is necessarily safe and sanitised but there is room to suggest that the drivers have become almost automatons cocooned away from the thought of danger. No such thing as changing gear with a lever after judging the optimum engine revs. Risk is relegated to the back of the shelf. Even the drivers on the last row of the grid are millionaires with management teams.

I remember the morning I arrived late for practice at a Belgian Grand Prix and asked that bearded doyen, Denis Jenkinson, who was quick. Jenks regarded me for a moment and said "They're *all* quick ... even the slow ones are quick." And of course the same stays true today if we are to assume that we watch the 20 best drivers in the world performing in a different country every fortnight with the action beamed by television to our living rooms wherever we may be in the world. The races may be excruciatingly clinical and boring to eyes that have been watching racing for half a century but this year I spoke to a young car salesman in New Zealand who had just returned from attending his first Grand Prix in Australia. His eyes were still like saucers and he spoke in awe of the noise and the enormity of the event.

So the excitement and the speed is still there to the fans who are always discovering the excitement of Grand Prix racing for the first time, and becoming the newly converted who can tell their mates about the glimpse of Michael Schumacher in the flesh.

I am pleased to have been involved in motor racing when there were what seemed like a handful of specialist journalists and photographers travelling from one race to another over the summer, mates with the drivers and the mechanics, when a post-race press conference was the driver sitting on the back tyre of his car and telling it like it had been during the previous few hours of sweaty track action.

Now there must be close to a thousand members of 'the media' who travel the world trying to write something different from their neighbour in the tabled ranks of writers, each with their mini TV screen. In 'my day' if you wanted to interview a driver, you asked him when it might be convenient to have a chat. They regarded an interview with enthusiasm because this was 'PR' (Public Relations) and an opportunity to get themselves and their opinions in print. Today a one-on-one interview with anyone on the front end of the grid is regarded as an imposition, an intolerable demand on a driver's time, and a seat in a crowded press conference is as near to an interview with a star driver as the average scribe is likely to get.

In 1955 the world of racing was a more leisurely place to be enjoyed at a more leisurely pace but the interpretations of what was actually happening often vary from book to book, journal to journal. Foreign races covered by local correspondents sometimes seemed like different events, comparing the various reports, and you can read interpretive angles on history as it was watched by the different reporters.

For all that, the amazing summer of 'fifty-five was just that. Amazing by any manner of rating. This book is my best effort at being there and taking the reader with me for a stroll down memory lane. I enjoyed the trip.

Eoin Young
*New Zealand*

# FOREWORD BY
# TONY BROOKS

*Formula 1 driver with Connaught, BRM, Vanwall, Ferrari
and Cooper. In 1955 he won the Syracuse Grand Prix
in a works Connaught, the first British driver to win
a Grand Prix in a British car for 32 years*

The author invites the reader to take a stroll down memory lane, recalling the events of the dramatic year that was 1955. I accepted the invitation and enjoyed the experience of being reminded of many events I had all but forgotten, learning about new information and stories despite being personally part of the racing scene that year.

The recounting of the exploits of the Siamese Prince 'B. Bira' really took me back in time, as it was his book *Bits & Pieces*, which recounted his adventures with his ERAs – *Romulus*, *Remus* and *Hanuman* – that first stirred my interest in motor racing, an innocent enough Christmas present ... or so my father thought!

The Le Mans and TT tragedies emphasised the danger of motor racing as never before, although precious little was done about it in the short term besides cancelling events. Today is a very different story. It is the virtual elimination of the risk of death or serious injury due to circuit design and the remarkable strength of the cars that is the dramatic difference between Grand Prix racing in 1955 and Formula 1 today.

The cars then raced on ordinary roads, or circuits that closely resembled them, lined with brick walls, ditches and trees, and drivers knew that any one mistake could be their last. The psychological challenge of trying to beat competitors given such a dangerous scenario was infinitely greater than today. This is just one reason why it is fatuous to compare the performances of today's drivers with those of the past who drove everything from saloon to Grand Prix cars on those circuits. Motor racing had to be made very much safer but it should be recognised that in achieving the incredible safety standards of today, the essence of motor racing in 1955 has been lost.

The author mentions Chris Amon and his suggestion that the Mercedes-Benz W196 was flattered by its drivers, Fangio and Moss, which it undoubtedly was, but putting them in works 250F Maseratis against the Mercedes would not have been the equivalent of removing Michael Schumacher from the Ferrari team in modern times. The percentage contribution the driver made to a winning car/driver combination in 1955 was so very much greater, not least because he was also responsible for all the driving performed by technology today. There are several drivers who could win the championship in Schumacher's championship winning Ferrari but that was not true for Mercedes in 1955, and Neubauer had the sense to recognise it.

Stirling Moss said that he learned to race from HWM and learned about life from Lance Macklin. He also took a free advanced driving course from Fangio, his tail-gating of the maestro prompting a rebuke from Mercedes. I can vouch for the fact that he learned all his lessons extremely well!

The author also covers Stirling's win in the Mille Miglia in some detail, for good reason. Averaging virtually 100mph around 1,000 miles of indifferent Italian roads that were supposed to be closed was one of his greatest driving performances. It would be fascinating to be able to borrow *Dr Who*'s telephone box and drop one of today's Formula 1 drivers into the driving seat of the 300SLR Mercedes on the starting ramp at Brescia at 7.22am that morning!

The author recounts the story about the Coventry Climax V8 2.5-litre engine. If only the firm had had the courage to persevere with the unit in 1953, motor racing history in subsequent years might well have read differently.

My Syracuse Connaught was a well-built car with good handling characteristics and was let down only by its Alta engine of pre-war design. The effort to extract more power, which still lagged behind its competitors, had prejudiced its durability; if a reliable Climax V8 had been available to Connaught, I have no doubt that it would have been a regular Grand Prix winner. The Alta engine with its limitations was my sole reason for turning down Connaught's invitation to drive for them in 1956.

The trip down memory lane is a pleasant meander, the author's easy, informative style making each turn of a page eagerly anticipated. It should be recommended reading for modern racing enthusiasts as well as those already steeped in the past as it will enable them to gain a better perspective about motor racing today.

# INTRODUCTION

1955. It was the worst and the best summer of international motor sport half a century ago. Stirling Moss won the Mille Miglia at record speed in a Mercedes 300SLR – averaging nearly 100mph for the 1,000 mile road race in Italy – and Tony Brooks won the Syracuse Grand Prix in a Connaught to become the first British driver in a British car to win a Grand Prix since Segrave won the San Sebastian Grand Prix in 1924. Brooks's race win was regarded as of such significance that *The Motor Yearbook* for 1956 was actually dedicated to Rodney Clarke, Managing Partner of Connaught Engineering.

Against those triumphs came tragedy when Bill Vukovich was killed at Indianapolis while aiming at what would have been a unique three-in-a-row hat-trick of wins in the famous 500-Mile Race. And at Le Mans a few weeks later a freak accident in front of the pits sent a Mercedes crashing at high speed and wreckage scything through the crowd killing more than 80. In the aftermath of that crash, races were cancelled across Europe. Mercedes-Benz had dominated Grand Prix and Sports Car races and when the company withdrew from racing at the end of the season, it was assumed that they were pulling out because of the Le Mans crash, but in fact Mercedes had announced before the season started that the summer of 'fifty-five would be their last in international motorsport.

It was an odd year. Mercedes had entered Grand Prix racing in 1954 in mid-season with a team of exciting W196 'streamliners' for the French Grand Prix at Reims with Juan Manuel Fangio as lead driver, and for 1955 Stirling Moss was signed to join the team. It seemed that the German dream team could not be beaten. But it would be.

Ferrari was in one of their downward swoops fielding ageing, updated 4-cylinder *Squalo* (shark) cars, Mercedes had their straight-eight W196s, the Maserati 250F was a six-cylinder, and the Lancia D50 was a V8. The French Gordini team flirted with their straight-eights without any real aim of success.

Looking back from our vantage point of 2005, the technology then seems scarcely worthy of the term. Blacksmith-ery is a better fit. But as ever in motor racing, any succeeding era is the ultimate in design. The best car with the best driver always wins.

In 1955 the best cars with the best drivers were undeniably Mercedes but years later Sir Stirling Moss would ruminate about the W196 and admit that it was not the easiest car he had ever driven in a Grand Prix. Ferrari were so far off the boil that they had seriously set about designing and building a *twin*-cylinder 2.5-litre engine for Monaco in the delusion that this would provide the instant low-speed punch needed to win on the street circuit. The fact that the prototype motor vibrated so badly that it tore up the test rig, probably saved a lot of face at Maranello.

Film star James Dean, sometime Porsche racer in California and star in *East of Eden, Rebel without a Cause* and

*Giant* was killed driving a Porsche in a road accident. Dean, 24, had promised the director of *Giant* that he would not risk injury by racing while the film was being made. Filming had finished and Dean was driving the Porsche spyder he had nicknamed *The Little Bastard* to a race at Salinas, California. He had already picked up a speeding ticket at Bakersfield where the cop apparently warned him that if he continued to drive at such speed on the public road he would never make the start of the race at Salinas. He didn't.

In the rest of the world, Bill Hayley's recording of *Rock Around the Clock* seemed like a hit in the making. *Cherry Pink and Apple Blossom White* topped the hit parade in Britain. Blue jeans were the new best-selling fashion for women. Eamon Andrews would compère a new television programme called *This is Your Life*. ITV would screen for the first time as opposition to BBC.

Five Formula 1 drivers were born in 1955: Alain Prost on 24th February, Rupert Keegan on 26th February, Teo Fabi on 9th March, Toshio Suzuki on 10th March and Philippe Strieff on 26th June.

Ray Kroc and Harland Sanders set about establishing the international fast food industry when Kroc bought a hamburger franchise from the McDonald brothers and Sanders started his Kentucky Fried Chicken franchise. Disneyland opened at Anaheim in California, the polio vaccine developed by microbiologist Jonas Salk was declared safe to use and Vladimir Nabakov published his naughty novel *Lolita*.

Princess Margaret sadly announced that she would not now be marrying Peter Townsend; the reason stated being that he was a formerly married man.

Donald Campbell put the Water Speed Record up to 202.32mph (325.53kph) in *Bluebird* on Ullswater in July and in November he upped the record again to 216.2mph (347.87kph).

Sir Winston Churchill, 80, retired as Prime Minister. I liked the story of one of his great grandchildren evading security and secretaries and getting access to Winston's gloomy office suite. "Is it true, great grand papa, that you are the greatest living Englishman?" asked the little lad. Sir Winston apparently considered the question, and then grumped "Yes ... now bugger off!"

Albert Einstein, 76, died.

Rootes took over Singer Motors.

The motor racing world was morbidly fascinated with the trial of Ruth Ellis for gunning down sometime racing driver, David Blakeley, with a Smith & Wesson revolver in London. She was hanged at Holloway Prison on August 24th, the last woman to be executed in Britain.

Citroën startled the Paris Motor Show with the radically different DS19; a car that was as new as their 21-year-old 11cv 'Maigret' model had been traditionally square and old-fashioned. Britain's show-stopper for the 1955 season was the new Jaguar 2.4-litre saloon that would evolve into the 3.4 and 3.8-litre cars to dominate the saloon car racing scene in future summers. Bentley announced the new Series 'S' to succeed the traditional Mark VI, mirrored in the Rolls-Royce Silver Cloud differing only in radiator style.

Volkswagen sold the millionth Beetle. Remember when the British Intelligence Sub-Committee did an investigation into Volkswagen and confidently forecast that the Beetle would never be a commercial success ...

By comparison, Mercedes sold the thousandth 300SL gull-wing coupé, with 93 per cent exported and over a dozen sent to Britain. Rob Walker was one of the first UK customers.

The Triumph TR3 sports car was announced, identical to the TR2 but for the egg-crate grille in the air intake and a space for a plus-one passenger behind the seats. A tool roll and tools were also included in the standard equipment of the TR3 which must have been an attractive selling feature.

In the US the first Road America races were run at Elkhart Lake and Phil Hill – "slender, high-strung, nimble witted, slyly humorous" – won the feature in his white Monza Ferrari by a few feet from Briggs Cunningham's D-type Jaguar driven by Sherwood Johnston – "big built, phlegmatic, easy going and a Scrooge with words".

Briggs Cunningham, the entrant who had invested hugely with dollars and enthusiasm to build an American winner in international sports car racing would soon announce that he was selling his Cunningham factory at West Palm Beach in Florida. He concentrated instead on campaigning British Jaguars and Italian Maseratis.

It was announced in December that Alex Issigonis, designer of the Morris Minor, was leaving the Alvis company where he had spent four years designing a new 3-litre saloon car which featured integral construction, a suspension system employing rubber which interconnected between front and rear to eliminate pitch ... but the project had been discontinued by Alvis chairman, J. J. Parkes, father of Michael Parkes who would grow up to be a prominent British racing driver and eventually manage the Ferrari team. And of course Issigonis would take his ideas to the British Motor Corporation to launch the runaway success of the Mini Minor.

Stirling Moss would win his first Grand Prix at Aintree in a Mercedes – the first Briton to win the British Grand Prix. Did he win, or did team-mate Fangio gift it to him? Speculation still poses the question but it seems fairly clear that Mercedes-Benz, comfortably in control of the summer's racing, suggested that Stirling take the laurels. Or, more specifically, suggested to Fangio that he finished second.

It seems hard to realise, 50 years down the track, that this was Stirling's first Grand Prix win. Surely he made history when he won in Argentina with Rob Walker's little Cooper? Correct, but that was three years later...

The Type 251 Bugatti was launched to a curious French press, fascinated by the fact that the pancake-shaped car featured the engine mounted transversely behind the driver. It lacked the lithe shape of the traditional pre-war Bugattis and would also lack the success when it appeared only once, in the 1956 French Grand Prix, and the brave project was then quietly shelved.

Tony Rolt, who shared the winning C-type Jaguar with Duncan Hamilton at Le Mans in 1953, announced his retirement from racing, to concentrate on a business with Harry Ferguson Research that championed four-wheel-drive and automatic transmission.

*Chapter 1*

# PRINCE 'BIRA' WINS IN NEW ZEALAND

The summer of '55 opened in New Zealand when the Siamese Prince 'B. Bira' won the Grand Prix on the Ardmore airfield circuit near Auckland in a 250F Maserati. It would be his last victory in a long and colourful career that had started at the Brooklands race track with a Riley Imp twenty years earlier. Prince Birabongse Bhanutej Bhanubandh of Thailand (formerly Siam) was born in 1914 and educated at Eton and Cambridge.

The matron of Eton shortened his name to 'Bira' and when he started racing in 1935 he entered as 'B. Bira'.

He lived in London with his cousin, Prince Chula Chakrabongse, where he studied sculpture under Charles Wheeler, RA, and would exhibit his work at the Royal Academy. In *Who's Who* Bira was described as: profession – sculptor; hobby – motor racing.

After the Riley came a racing MG Magnette and on his 21st birthday, Chula presented him with an ERA 1.5-litre *voiturette* single-seater which he christened *Romulus*. He finished second in his first race at Dieppe, beaten by South African driver Pat Fairfield. When Fairfield was killed in a crash at Le Mans in 1937 Bira sculpted a tribute that would be exhibited at the British Racing Drivers' Club.

Chula decided to manage his cousin's racing affairs and they started The White Mouse Stable run on professional lines. He foxed the opposition with pit signals in Siamese. They raced a succession of ERAs, christened *Remus* and *Hanuman*. Bira's first Maserati was the 8CM with its distinctive heart-shaped radiator cowl originally raced by Whitney Straight.

He would win the BRDC Road Racing Gold Star in 1936, 1937 and 1938 which made him virtually British Champion in each of those years. In 1939 he raced in blue and yellow Siamese racing colours. A measure of Bira's ability was the fact that he won a third of all the pre-war races won by ERAs and beat team patron, Raymond Mays, in a straight fight at Brooklands in 1936. He also won the *voiturette* race at Monaco that year.

It was not generally known that Bira had measles as a boy and the infection left him with poor eyesight. Although there were few photographs of the prince wearing spectacles, he always wore goggles with prescription lenses.

Bira wrote a delightfully naïve motor racing autobiography *Bits & Pieces* in 1942 which included his description of his first visit to Le Mans in 1935, passing up dessert at the Hotel de Paris to drive to the circuit for night practice. "I put down the hood on my Vanden Plas sports-tourer and fixed some small aero screens in front of us, after having folded down the big windscreen. In the dim light, being only partially lit up by a few electric lights, the blue Bentley looked quite racy. To add further to the sporting appearance I also pulled up the exhaust lever, this letting out the less muffled exhaust note of the "silent sports-car". The Bentley was 'racy' enough and noisy enough to be waved through on to the circuit by gendarmes at a road block. Chula was terrified and asked to be dropped at the pits and Bira continued unchecked. "This time I did get quite a fair speed out of the Bentley, and I occasionally glanced at the speedometer. The dial showed that the car was travelling between ninety-six and ninety-eight miles an hour. That speed from a non-tuned up and fully-equipped car, was not bad at all. Indeed I was very pleased with the performance and also the way it clung to the road along the twisty bits. I realised then more fully than ever that if British engineers had been given the chance to design some real Grand Prix racing machines, they would have shown the world something, and would have given some real competition to the Mercedes and the Auto-Union, for without doubt the E.R.A. has already done much in the light car class."

It seems difficult to grasp in this modern safety conscious age but Bira stayed out on the course and was mixing it for several laps with an Alfa Romeo. When he finally stopped at the pits, Chula told him he had been dicing with Raymond Sommer. "What! Sommer? The French ace?' I exclaimed." This was period *Boy's Own Paper* adventure and by further chance, Sommer invited Bira to share a shapely works-supplied 2.6-litre unblown Alfa Romeo coupé at Le Mans in 1939. They suffered engine problems (Sommer took the head off and changed a gasket in the pits!), a puncture and eventually terminal overheating.

On fitness as a driver, Bira wrote "The best way of keeping oneself up to the mark, is to keep happy and not to worry about anything or anybody. When one gets into a motorcar one should drive it as best one can. I did not deny myself any weakness or fun if I happened to feel like it." The Prince also had a fascinating attitude to finance. When Chula said he was planning to give him £1,000 for his birthday, Bira listed all the things he would like to buy that cost around £1,000 – and went out and bought them *all*!

In 1947 he was racing another Maserati, this time a 1.5-litre 4CL model which he drove to win at Chimay in France. In 1948 he won the first-ever race on the Zandvoort circuit in Holland in a new 4CLT/48 super-charged Maserati and he led the 1949 British GP at Silverstone before retiring. He was also picked for the team to race the new XK120 Jaguars in the Production Car race at Silverstone at that year's *Daily Express* International Trophy Meeting and led for the first half hour before a tyre blew. By 1951 he was racing a Maserati fitted with a 4.5-litre Osca engine but the hybrid was not a success.

In 1952/53 he flew to Bangkok and back in his Miles Gemini aircraft and in 1954 he was back at Maserati placing an order for the sleek new 250F 2.5-litre six-cylinder Grand Prix car. His order was fourth to be received and he was allotted chassis and engine number 2504. To pacify the impatient prince who discovered that his 250F would not in fact be ready until the June of 1954 after the factory cars had been sorted out, Maserati decided to fit the 250F engine into a Formula 2 chassis raced the previous season. This interim model was known as the A6 GCM and Bira drove it to win again in the *GP de Frontières* at Chimay. When the customer 250F space-frames finally started coming through, Bira's engine was matched up with chassis 2504 for the first time.

He raced in several GPs that season with a best finish of fourth in the French GP at Reims. At the end of the season he shipped the 250F to New Zealand for the 1955 Grand Prix on January 8th. The race was to be held for the second time on the Ardmore airfield circuit south of Auckland. The previous year the race had been won by Stan Jones in his Maybach Special. His son Alan would win the World Championship for the Williams team in 1980.

In fact Bira also shipped his unloved and unlovely Osca-Maserati to New Zealand in the hope of finding a buyer in the colonies. This was a car built up from his 4CLT chassis fitted with the 4.5-litre V12 Osca engine. He eventually sold it in Australia.

Main opposition came from the pair of special Ferraris entered by Peter Whitehead and Tony Gaze. These were Tipo 500 chassis fitted with 3-litre sports car engines for extra performance and, more importantly so far from home, reliability. The Gaze chassis was the one raced by Alberto Ascari when he won the world title in 1952 and 1953.

The Grand Prix grid was supposedly decided from the results of two 12-lap qualifying heats but while Whitehead won his heat at a faster time than Bira's in winning the second heat, the Prince was awarded pole position for the race. Not that it made much difference when the flag fell. By the end of the first lap Bira was in a lead he never lost despite fading brakes late in the race. He was slowing with the gearbox and getting as hard on the brakes as he was able.

There was a theory that Whitehead and Gaze were banking on Bira making a pitstop, but he ran though non-stop and Whitehead and Gaze followed him in second and third.

With suitable colonial irreverence, Bira was nicknamed 'The Drain Layer' after being late to the grid, having reportedly been pleasuring his lady friend in the privacy of a dry drainage ditch behind the paddock.

Other runners in the Grand Prix included a youthful Jack Brabham who was placed fourth in his Cooper Bristol, two laps adrift. Bruce McLaren's father, Les, retired his Austin-Healey 100/4 after 30 laps.

After finishing third to Peter Collins and Roy Salvadori in a 250F 1–2–3 back at Silverstone in May, Bira announced his retirement and sold the Maserati to British privateer, Horace Gould.

Bira enjoyed yachting, representing Thailand in the 1955 Melbourne Olympics, visiting his old motor racing friends at the first international races on the Albert Park circuit. He was also in the Olympic team in 1972. He was flying and gliding and involved himself in an airline business back home in Thailand but fate dealt him poor cards, and he was eventually found destitute and dead on the Underground platform at Barons Court in London two days before Christmas in 1985. He was 71.

*Chapter 2*

# THOSE SEARING SOUTH AMERICAN RACES

The Grand Prix in Argentina in January was the season-opening showdown that would pit Mercedes with Fangio and Moss against Lancia with Ascari, Villoresi and Castellotti, Ferrari with Gonzalez, Farina and Maglioli and Maserati with Behra, Musso, Mantovani and Mières. Mercedes also fielded cars for German drivers Kling and Herrmann but it was clear that Fangio and Moss were expected to be the team's frontline runners. This race would obviously be the indicator of 1955 form. There were seven Maseratis in total, with Harry Schell, Carlos Menditeguy and Clemar Bucci as private entries. Three French Gordinis were entered for Elie Bayol, Pablo Birger and Jesus Iglesias.

The German team had been bested in the final Grand Prix of 1954 and for the new season the W196s had been shortened and shed 70kg. The fuel injection system had been revised and power was now up over 280bhp. Mindful of the grilles being blocked with stray paper on the course as happened in Spain the previous season, a spring-loaded hinged grille had been fixed across the radiator air intake with a cockpit lever so that the driver could flick the grille and clear any litter blockage on command from the pit.

Mercedes shipped five cars and flew the engines straight from the test bed in Germany for installation in Buenos Aires. In fact they were on a two-race campaign as a Formule Libre race was scheduled for a fortnight after the Grand Prix on a different circuit within the same complex. It seems that Mercedes may have been instrumental in the listing of the open-formula race since Fangio was on home ground and enthusiasm seemed limitless with obvious marketing appeal for Mercedes. The company also saw the second event as an opportunity to race-test their new 3-litre engines to be used in the 300SLR sports-racers which were directly based on the W196, virtually two-seater versions of the Grand Prix cars with bigger and more powerful engines.

Lancia saw the South American Grand Prix as an important season indicator and took the unprecedented step of sending all their cars, drivers, team management and mechanics by air, chartering a Douglas DC6 from KLM.

The D50s in 1955 form were proving a handful for even Ascari who suffered the embarrassment of several spins during the week of practice, when they ran in the early evenings to try and avoid the searing heat of the day.

In fact it would be a different local driver who commanded qualifying when the stocky Froilan Gonzalez, nicknamed 'The Pampas Bull', put his blue-and-yellow Ferrari in Argentine racing colours on pole at 1min 43.1sec, half a second faster than Ascari and Fangio who had tied on 1min 43.6sec in the Lancia and Mercedes respectively. Behra's Maserati, on 1min 43.8sec, completed a front row of four different marques indicating an interesting season to come. But the interest would wane almost from flag-fall.

Farina, Kling and Schell lined up Ferrari–Mercedes–Maserati on the second row, continuing the marque variety. Farina was racing for the first time since being badly burned in a sports car accident the previous season and his legs were swathed in asbestos to try and keep cool. A doctor administered morphine to the 1950 World Champion just before the start. Moss was back on row three.

If the teams had practised late in the day to dodge the heat, there was no escape from the sun on race day. It was 95°F as the cars took the grid for the 4pm start and the 96-lap Grand Prix was scheduled to run for three hours.

Fangio was an immediate leader from the start with Gonzalez and Ascari disputing second place. Moss was coming through strongly. Three laps gone and Ascari was leading in the Lancia, its handling apparently better on full tanks than in low-fuel qualifying trim. Three laps gone and so were Behra's Maserati, Kling's Mercedes, Birger's Gordini and Menditeguy's Maserati. Behra had spun his Maserati while trying to pass Schell, and had come back on track to clout Kling's Mercedes which was then collected by the others. Villoresi had spun his Lancia when the engine cut with a carburation problem and he also retired. Behra stepped straight into Mantovani's 250F, the first of many cockpit-swaps in this race. Castellotti had given up, exhausted in the heat and Villoresi took over his Lancia.

Gonzalez was briefly leading from Ascari on lap nine with Fangio and Moss pacing themselves behind the hectic action out in front. Ascari speared through safety fences on the 20th lap and was then another retirement with the nose of the D50 stove in. Gonzalez was now back in front in the Ferrari, 15sec clear of Fangio and Moss in the two silver Mercedes with Schell (Maserati) and Herrmann (Mercedes) in fourth and fifth.

Fangio was reading the race correctly. Gonzalez had flayed himself out in front and pitted in exhaustion exacerbated by pain from injuries received in a crash the previous season. The musical-chairs charade continued. Froilan was heaved out of the Ferrari and Farina climbed in to take over while Maglioli stepped into Farina's abandoned car...

Fangio and Moss were now running first and second but all was not what it might have seemed. Moss's Mercedes stuttered to a stop on lap 29 with a vapour lock in the fuel system. Stirling climbed out and collapsed on the grass. An ambulance arrived and Stirling was bundled in, protesting that he was only exhausted, not injured, and he was eventually delivered to the Mercedes pit.

Three laps later and Fangio was rolling down the pit lane to be greeted by team manager Neubauer asking why he had stopped. Fangio, confused and exhausted, said he had no idea why he had stopped. Neubauer solved the situation by tossing buckets of water over his driver, who continued more or less refreshed, back into the heat of race.

Moss was also sluiced down and sent back into the race in the Mercedes that had already been driven by Herrmann and Kling, to finish fourth.

Fangio went on to win the race, one of only two drivers (the other was fellow Argentine Mières, who finished fifth in the Maserati) to complete the race single-handed.

The results, with all the shared cars, were so complex that Farina and Trintignant were both officially listed as finishing second *and* third! The second-placed Ferrari was driven at various stages of the race, by Gonzalez–Farina–Trintignant and the third-placed Ferrari was shared by Farina–Trintignant–Maglioli.

Fangio would recall that hectic race in his memoirs: "I was at the end of my tether. I won that race simply by staying in the car." His leg was burning against a hot chassis tube and he would carry the angry scar for the rest of his days. "To stop myself from passing out, I tried to imagine that I was lost in the snow, and that I had to keep going or I would die of cold. There was a time when I thought I couldn't do it but then my morale came back, and the will to win. When it was all over they had to lift me out of the car. They laid me on the floor of the pits and gave me an injection." He was too exhausted to attend the victory celebrations that evening and a doctor the next day diagnosed heart strain.

A fortnight later the teams were at the track again for the Formule Libre race on a different course layout. The Lancia team were absent, having returned to their Turin base to lick various wounds and try and address the problem of instability when the distinctive pannier tanks between the wheels were low on fuel. Ferrari had comfortably fitted a 3-litre 750S sports car engine in Farina's Grand Prix chassis but the Mercedes 300SLR engine had to sit more upright in the chassis than its 2.5-litre counterpart and a new bulging bonnet was fitted. To fight the effects of the heat they had suffered in the Grand Prix a fortnight before, both cars were fitted with scoops and tubes to try and cool the drivers.

Trintignant and Gonzalez were driving their 2.5-litre Grand Prix Ferraris and Maglioli was entered in a 750S Ferrari sports-racer as befitted the anything-goes open-formula race. The two 250F Maseratis were running 2.7-litre motors.

There were to be two heats of 30 laps with aggregate times deciding the results. Neubauer made a rare error on tyre choice and the first heat went to Farina's Ferrari, although Moss and then Fangio had been leading. The second heat was a mirror of the first with Fangio and Moss out in front, but in the closing laps Trintignant closed up in the Ferrari and Moss rushed past Fangio to escape the unwelcome attention of the Frenchman and crossed the line to win his first race for Mercedes. When the race times were added, however, Fangio emerged the leader with Moss second and the Ferrari shared by Gonzalez and Trintignant in third place.

The teams now returned to Europe for the long wait until the next round of the World Championship at Monaco in May.

*Chapter 3*

# THE SAGA OF RUTH ELLIS AND DAVID BLAKELEY

The four bullets in his body lying on the footpath outside the Magdala pub in Hampstead on the Easter Sunday of 1955 made David Blakeley a good deal more famous than he could ever hope to have been as a racing driver. He had been shot to death by peroxide-blonde prostitute, Ruth Ellis, who was convicted of murdering her on-off boyfriend and became the last woman to be executed in Britain.

The trial and subsequent execution became a headliner event with everyone involved getting their few moments of fame. Even the official hangman, Albert Pierrepoint, described as a semi-literate Manchester publican who earned £15 for every execution, was interviewed after the event. "She was no trouble. She wobbled a bit, naturally. Any woman can do that. Nothing wrong with her. She was as good as gold, she was." Before the death penalty was abolished in Britain, Pierrepoint hanged a total of 520 men and women. Ruth requested and drank a brandy before she met her end. Her daughter Georgie would write in her book *Ruth Ellis, My Mother* published in 1995, that men had been known to ejaculate, vomit and defecate in their last moment. "I doubt if my mother had an orgasm as her ultimate human experience, but it would be nice to believe that she did." Books were written on Ruth and a movie *Dance with a Stranger* was made in 1985 with Miranda Richardson as Ruth and Rupert Everett as Blakeley. An appeal in 2003 by Ellis's 82-year-old sister was dismissed, the appeal judges stating that she had been properly convicted of murder as the law stood at the time.

Both Ellis and Blakeley loved each other, hated each other, drank to excess and fought. Ten days before the murder Ellis had suffered a miscarriage after Blakeley, the baby's father, punched her violently in the stomach. Ruth was known politely as a club hostess but an enthusiastic queue of customers would claim she put her popularity on a professional basis. Daughter Georgie would record in her book "She employed a different language, one in which the word fuck was the most useful verb and noun, and its accompanying participle, fucking, served her well as both adverb and adjective."

Blakeley was a Yorkshireman, born in Sheffield in 1929, the son of a doctor, who, in a curious twist to this tale was tried for the murder of a '25-year-old unemployed waitress' by injecting her with a pituitrin-based drug to abort his baby. The trial was dismissed on the grounds that the evidence against Dr Blakeley was so weak. The good Doctor's good-time habits eventually resulted in divorce and David went to live with his mother who would shortly marry Humphrey Cook, a wealthy man from an old-established family drapery business. It was Cook who sowed the seeds of motor racing enthusiasm in young David who was ten-years old when his mother remarried.

Cook had been a prominent racing driver, competing at Brooklands from 1914 to 1937. He competed in a black and red 30/98 Vauxhall known as *Rouge et Noir* and in 1923 when he bought one of the 1922 TT Vauxhalls he named it *Rouge et Noir II*. He asked Amherst Villiers to super-charge the Vauxhall and this would become the basis for Raymond Mays's Vauxhall-Villiers sprint and hill climb car. Mays would appear later in the Cook career. He crashed a works Aston Martin at Brooklands in 1925 after the steering failed and he also raced the slimline *Razor Blade* Aston Martin special which, to this day, appears in pride of place on the British Racing Drivers' Club badge. Mays persuaded Cook to finance the formation of the E.R.A. (English Racing Automobiles) company to build *voiturette* single-seaters with Riley-based engines and run a works team. This idea appealed to Cook who had been eager to build a car of his own but lacked the expertise. He invested £75,000 in the new company and he entered the first ERA in the 1934 BRDC British Empire Trophy at Brooklands, and he also scored the marque's first win in a Brooklands Mountain Handicap.

Cook funded his stepson to public school at Shrewsbury where he learned little as a loner who immersed himself in motor racing, reading all the magazines of the day and fuelling an interest that would become an obsession. When he left school in the post-war years there were no jobs in motor racing so Cook, who was at home in Mayfair society, arranged for Blakeley to be trained in hotel management at the Hyde Park Hotel. It seems that the job did not appeal but the available attrac-tion of wealthy ladies at the expensive hotel eager for male company, as well as the ever-open bars, began his enthusiasm for sex and drinking. It was an enthusiasm that would lead to his end.

It was a matter of proximity that propelled David Blakeley into the company of the upper echelons of motor racing. The Steering Wheel Club, the popular watering hole for motor-sporting folk, was just a ten-minute walk from the Hyde Park Hotel. Stirling Moss, Peter Collins and Mike Hawthorn were regulars at 'The Wheel' and Blakeley bought his way on to the fringe of their company but like so many wannabes he was out of his depth. Battles with soda siphons were popular among drinkers in the 'fifties and Blakeley made a major error of judgement one evening when he emptied a bucket of ice over Hawthorn and then squirted soda at him. Hawthorn, apparently, took this jape by a drunken twerp rather badly. Georgie noted in her book "Hawthorn reacted violently and if others had not intervened would probably have killed him, thereby saving Ruth the trouble later on!"

When his doctor father died, David inherited a substantial amount of money and went on a spending spree. Humphrey Cook had bought his stepson an HRG sports car. One of his affairs of the heart was with Carol Findlater whom he met via an advertisement that her husband had placed to sell an old Alfa Romeo. Anthony Findlater was the son of pre-war racer, Seaton Findlater and the two men – Blakeley and 'Ant' as Anthony was known – would eventually work together on a project to build a stylish sports-racer to be called the Emperor. In the meantime Blakeley enjoyed talking motor racing with Mr Findlater … and bedding his wife. Ruth Ellis came into the equation soon after.

Cliff Davis was another racing driver of club note and popular at 'The Wheel'. He knew both Blakeley and Ellis and Georgie noted that Cliff was one of the few people to speak up for Ruth as a person … aside from her sexual activities. "He held her in high regard as a woman of principle. In contrast he found Blakeley a man of few principles. As a pair, he felt it was a tragedy they had ever met and described their relationship as being as unstable as a stick of dynamite." When Cliff first met Blakeley, he was describing Ruth as "the best fuck in London".

Ant Findlater worked for Aston Martin but Blakeley persuaded him to come and work full-time on the Emperor project. This stopped the day that Humphrey Cook told his step-son that he was cutting off his allowance. Blakeley must have had some talent at the wheel and was a reserve driver with the Bristol team at Le Mans and Rheims in 1954. In August 1954 he was racing a friend's MG at Zandvoort.

The Emperor was eventually completed. It was powered by a 1,500cc Singer engine with HRG twin-cam heads, a de Dion rear end and Volkswagen front suspension. The car looked stylish and Blakeley entered it in the Kent Cup for sports cars up to 1,500cc on the first-ever Boxing Day race meeting at Brands Hatch in 1954. A youthful Stirling Moss was disguised as Father Christmas. A photograph in *Autosport* shows Blakeley in the Emperor, lapping John Aley's HRG. The race report said: "Three quarters of a minute separated Coombs and Blakeley when the flag fell, but it was a splendid debut for the promising new Emperor." John Coombs won the race in his Connaught-engined Lotus, Blakeley was second in the Emperor and

Nigel Allen (father of James, ITV Grand Prix commentator) was third in a Lotus-MG.

Early in 1955 Ruth was volunteering to take French lessons so that she could impress Blakeley when he took her to Le Mans, as he had promised. It never happened. Their drunken arguments and their wild affairs with others between or because of these arguments continued and one of Ruth's men-friends provided her with a .38 Smith & Wesson six-shot black revolver.

On the night of Easter Sunday, April 10, an irate Ruth, now fuelled by Pernod, set out to find her unfaithful lover. She discovered his Vanguard outside the Magdala pub and waited for him to come out. She called out his name twice and when he looked across at her she fired two shots. He started to run but a third shot hit and felled him. She fired a fourth shot from several paces and then another into his back from point-blank range of a few inches. She put the barrel to her head to kill herself with the one remaining bullet but changed her mind, fired wildly and the ricochet hit the thumb of a woman strolling to the pub for a drink with her banker husband.

By a quirk of fate, the killing that would have made headlines the next morning, never reached the streets of London for eleven days because of a national newspaper strike. The morning after the trial eventually started, headlines in Fleet Street screamed *MODEL SHOT CAR ACE IN BACK*. The jury took 23 minutes to reach their verdict. Ruth Ellis was found guilty and hanged thirteen weeks and three days after the fatal shooting.

## Chapter 4

# MOSS AND THE
# MILLE MIGLIA –
# 1,000 MILES AT 100MPH!

Why did the Italians name the Mille Miglia – the most prestigious motor race in their history – in miles instead of kilometres? The loquacious Count Giovanni (Johnny) Lurani, who lived in some style near Monza in a gracious villa with a multi-car garage papered with posters from 1930s GPs he had raced in, explains: "The four men who devised the race, Count Aymo Maggi, Count Franco Mazzotti, Renzo Castagneto and Giovanni Canestrini, were discussing a name for their event when Mazzotti was asked about the length of the course and was told it was 1,600 kilometres. Having just returned from America, Mazzotti converted that to one thousand miles and suggested the name Coppa della Mille Miglia. One of the others thought that the Anglo-Saxon measure-ment might offend some political zealot but Mazzotti pointed out that the Romans measured their distances in miles and therefore they were following Roman tradition. The first announcement of the event was published in *Gazzetta dello Sport* on 4th December 1926.

If Fangio was the acknowledged master of Formula 1 with two world titles already to his credit by 1955 and three more to come, the 25-year-old Stirling Moss was the master in sports car racing. In the Mercedes 300SLR sports-racer that made its competition debut in that summer of 'fifty-five, he would win the world title for Mercedes with long-distance victories in the Mille Miglia, the Swedish Grand Prix (held that year for sports cars), the Tourist Trophy race at Dundrod in Northern Ireland and the Targa Florio. But his greatest win that summer, perhaps the greatest win of his career, was in the Mille Miglia. It was his fifth attempt and his first finish. He won from Fangio by just over half an hour at a record average speed of 97.93mph (157.57kph). For the first time the classic had been won by an Englishman and it was the second time it had been won by a non-Italian car. By chance, the first was Caracciola in 1931 also in a Mercedes. Moss increased the race average speed by almost 10mph!

The photograph at the finish is etched in racing history. A young Moss with his white overalls wearing only the emblem of the British Racing Drivers' Club and his personal badge embroidered with his SM initials. He wore a black body belt and he looked a mixture between exhaustion and elation. Denis Jenkinson wore a happy smile, relieved perhaps that their plans to cope with the impossibilities of the long race had been rewarded with the win. Both faces were begrimed around where their goggles had framed tired eyes in black dust.

The race was over 1,000 miles (992m – 1,596km to be exact) of public roads from Brescia eastward across the Lombardy plain to Verona and Padua then south to Ferrara and Ravenna. There were long open straights down to Ancona on the Adriatic coast then well south to

Pescara where the race hooked west through the Abruzzi mountains to half distance at Rome. The course then ran north to Siena and into the hairpins of the Apennines and the Futa Pass to Bologna, down through Piacenza and Cremona, across the Po river, passing Nuvolari's home town of Mantua and back to Brescia. There was a special speed prize for the Cremona/Mantua section in Nuvolari's name.

*The Autocar* endeavoured to compare the epic race to a drive that readers could relate to in Britain. "Imagine having an early breakfast and leaving London by car at about 7.15am, reaching Aberdeen by lunchtime and getting back to London in time for a latish tea – with only two stops. That, on roads that are admittedly better than British roads, parallels the achievement of Stirling Moss last weekend in winning the 22nd Mille Miglia. Sometimes his car was reaching nearly 170mph (274kph) on the straight, but the roads are narrow and lined with concrete posts. The race took place in blazing sunshine. Moss's companion was bearded Dennis [sic] Jenkinson, well known in another sphere as an ace sidecar rider."

The roads were closed for a night and a day, opening along its length as the last car passed through.

The cars started a minute apart and the first car left at 9.00pm on the Saturday night. Their race numbers were their start times, drawn by ballot according to class and category. Moss's Mercedes was number 722 indicating his start time at 7.22am the following morning. The tiddlers at the head of the field included tiny Fiat Topolinos and 2CV Citroëns. First away was a Fiat in a new category for diesel-engined cars.

The 300SLR was essentially a two-seater version of the W196 Grand Prix cars with the straight-eight engine increased from 2.5-litres to 3-litres with a square bore and stroke. It had fuel injection, dual ignition, dry sump lubrication and desmodromic mechanically-operated valves. The five-speed transmission had synchromesh on second to fifth gears. Suspension was by torsion bars with swing axles at the rear.

The Mercedes entry included German drivers Karl Kling and Hans Herrmann as well as Fangio and Moss. Kling was said to have covered several thousand miles in practice laps of the course on open roads but he crashed just before Rome, around half distance, and broke three of his ribs.

Fangio drove alone, citing the fact that a co-driver friend had been killed when he had crashed years before in a long-distance race in Argentina. Moss chose Denis Jenkinson to ride with him, not as a co-driver but very much as a specialist navigator who was accustomed to speed, having ridden as a sidecar passenger – as *The Autocar* correspondent explained – to motorcycle racer Eric Oliver when he was winning World Championships on European circuits in the late 1940s. He also had prior experience of the Mille Miglia from the passenger's seat, partnering George Abecassis in an HWM the previous year. Jenks was ideal for the job: small, wiry and apparently fearless. He was known to his legion of readers as 'D.S.J.' at the foot of his reports and columns in *Motor Sport*, the monthly 'bible' which began in the 1920s and still dominates the monthly motor sporting press. He was known as 'Jenks' to his friends and he made sure that these friends were carefully vetted circles in a small variety of areas, because he was also eagerly involved in vintage motorcycle racing and vintage cars. I was fortunate enough to be included in what he called his Gang of Five among motorsport journalists – Alan Henry, Nigel Roebuck, Maurice Hamilton, myself and himself. It was a tight-knit club and we were proud to be members.

Jenks had ridden thousands of rapid miles with Moss around the Mille Miglia course while the roads were open, making notes of corners, their severity, direction, following blind hazards, and an agreed reckoning of maximum pace at which they would be 'do-able' at speed when the roads were closed and the Great Race was on. These notes were strung together on a sheet of special paper 18-feet long.

For their first *recce* lap they were given a prototype 300SLR with instructions not to exceed 170mph (274kph) in fifth gear, to always fill the tank with Agip *Supercortemaggiore* petrol, not to hurry (!), to take two days over completing the first lap and not to drive in the dark. Kling and Herrmann followed them in a 220 Mercedes saloon and another car was full of technicians and mechanics.

"Moss soon found that this *rennsportwagen*, as the Germans so aptly name this type of machine, was quite happy cruising between 145 and 155mph (233 to 250kph) amid the general run of Italian traffic. The acceleration from 50 to 150mph (80 to 241kph) gave the feeling of being absolutely constant, there was no kick in the back, no sudden surge forward, but a constant increase of speed, while the suspension was so comfortable and the road-holding such that the rev counter reading and gear-lever position were the only guides to the speed.

"I made copious notes, some of them rather like Chinese due to trying to write at 150mph but when we stopped for lunch or for the night, we spent the whole time discussing the roads we had covered and transcribing my notes," Jenks wrote in *Motor Sport*. "The things we concentrated on were places where we might break the car, such as very bumpy railway crossings, sudden dips in the road, bad surfaces, tramlines and so on. Then we logged all the difficult corners, grading them as 'saucy ones,' 'dodgy ones,' and 'very dangerous ones,' having a hand sign to indicate each type. Then we logged slippery surfaces, using another hand sign, and as we went along Moss indicated his interpretation of the conditions, while I pin-pointed the place by a kilometre stone, plus or minus. Our task was eased greatly by the fact that there is a stone at every kilometre on Italian roads, and they are numbered in huge black figures, facing oncoming traffic."

They did more days of testing around the course dealing with the everyday Italian traffic. "Moss had sufficient confidence in me to take blind brows at 90–100mph, believing me when I said the road went straight on; though he freely admitted that he was not sure whether he would do the same thing at 170mph in the race, no matter how confident I was. He said he'd probably ease it back to 160mph, for though that 10mph would make no difference to the resulting crash if I had made a mistake, it comforted him psychologically!"

In Ken Purdy's book *All But My Life*, Moss said "I might have finished the race without Denis Jenkinson, although I doubt it, but I couldn't possibly have *won* without him." The italics are mine. I thought Stirling himself would have stressed the point about the race *win*. Moss went on to tell Purdy, "Denis told me that because he knew that he could not handle a 300SLR at that speed, that it was beyond him and foreign to his experience, he wasn't frightened; but that had I been driving a Porsche, which he knows, and which he can drive very well himself, then he'd have been badly frightened. As for me, no amount of money, nothing, would persuade me to sit for ten hours in a car that somebody else was driving at 170 miles an hour over blind brows. The very thought of it frightens me ..."

On their first trial lap among Italian commuters, Jenks noted that while they were not going at racing Mille Miglia speeds, Moss refused to take any chances. At no time did he use more than his own half of the road and never squeezing through gaps but they were still averaging over 90mph (145kph) including obeying traffic lights and going round the traffic islands.

In his book *A Story of Formula 1* written five years later in 1960, Jenks recalled Fangio setting off for his first trial run from the Hotel Brescia. "Fangio had set off that morning in the practice 300SLR and the general rule was that when doing a practice lap of the 1,000-mile course, one went on until dusk and then stopped at a convenient hotel. When I met him looking very tired and dirty it was about 9pm and darkness had fallen some three hours before so I was amazed to see him back in Brescia. After he had bathed and joined us at supper he explained that he had made excellent time round the circuit. Darkness was beginning to fall as he reached

Modena but knowing the route from there to Brescia very well he decided to press on after dark and complete the whole lap in one day, but as he battled his way up the Via Emilia amid the lorries, scooters and inevitable Fiats he found that the 300SLR had only one headlamp working and he had completely under-estimated the traffic. His description of the nightmare drive in a racing Mercedes-Benz with only one headlamp amid the evening traffic of Italy did not leave anything to the imagination and explained why he had arrived in the hotel looking very haggard and worn ..."

The second lap the following day was very different. "After averaging 95mph for the first hour and a half, fate stepped in and it is best that a veil is drawn over the details. First the rain came, then a stone punctured the radiator, and after the mechanics had rushed another one to us and fitted it, the snow started. We struggled on for another 200 miles in weather conditions which ranged from hail to three inches of slush on the roads, with ice forming on the windscreen and goggles faster than we could rub it off. Nearing Rome the weather cleared up and conditions were perfect once again, but shortly after Rome we were passing a flock of sheep at 70mph when the attendant shepherd struck one of them with a hefty stick and it leapt sideways into our left-hand headlamp. While the dead mutton flew up into the air, we spun and, in going into the ditch, a rear wheel struck a low concrete bollard and that was that ..." They finished the lap in the 220 Mercedes saloon with Kling and Herrmann.

Stirling had an alloy case made for Jenks's map-roller system. "For our final practice I employed this machine, winding the paper from the lower roller to the upper one, the notes being read through a Perspex window, sealed with Sellotape, in the event of the race being run in rain."

Because of its obvious comparison to a roll of toilet paper, it was forever known as 'The Loo Roll'. It was not Jenks's brainchild (photographer Louis Klemantaski had used a similar method in earlier Mille Miglias) and he had discussed such a roller-map with the American driver, John Fitch, when it seemed that he might drive with him in the 1955 race. That was before Moss telephoned and asked him to ride with him in the Mercedes. Jenks perfected the 'loo roll' and history will always recognise him as its creator.

The main opposition came from Ferraris driven by Piero Taruffi, Umberto Maglioli and Paolo Marzotto in 3.75-litre cars and Castellotti in a brand new un-raced 300bhp 4.4-litre 'Indianapolis' model. Peter Collins led the British entries in a DB3S Aston Martin and there were four of the new 100S Austin-Healeys for car-maker Donald Healey, Lance Macklin, George Abecassis and Ron Flockhart.

Italy lived for the Mille Miglia. "The fascination of this principal Italian sports car race has several sources, not the least of which is the enthusiasm and extraordinary motoring knowledge of the people of the country." wrote *The Autocar*'s correspondent, painting in the colourful background. "Throughout the race every Italian-owned television set and radio is tuned to the event and the latest news of the leading cars is exchanged in the street between strangers, excitedly passed on to customers by restaurant waiters, and vigorously debated in almost every public place."

At Ravenna, Pescara, Rome, Florence and Bologna there were Mercedes-Benz pits complete with all spares, changes of tyres should it start to rain, food, drink and assistance of every sort, for in this race there were no complicated rules about work done on the car or outside assistance. It was a free-for all!

While Moss would blitz the event, they had not considered their chances of winning as the race started. Jenks: "We fully expected Fangio to set the pace with Kling determined to win at all costs, so we were out for a third place and to beat all the Ferraris." It was popularly supposed among the journalists in the Press bars in Brescia and beyond that Alfred Neubauer, Mercedes team manager, was sending the Moss car out to break the pace of the bigger and presumably faster Ferraris, and that Fangio would be the designated winner as he had been all season in Formula 1.

This may or may not have been the case because Moss knew only one speed once the flag dropped and they were storming down off the ramp, having been told by Neubauer that they could clear the base of the ramp under acceleration without bottoming.

The man from *The Autocar* was stationed on the course with friends further around its length to phone in coverage of a race that was impossible to report from only one point. "Moss arrived at a tricky left-hander on the tail of a Ferrari and took the corner visibly faster than any other competitor, even including Fangio, stilling the crowd to momentary silence before excitement broke out again as the Mercedes went on to overtake the Ferrari in the next bend.

"Among the fastest cars Moss was soon in the lead. At Ancona (on the Adriatic coast, about one-third distance)

Taruffi was but 34sec behind in a Ferrari which had started last. Then came the Mercedes 300SLR of Hans Herrmann, Castellotti's Ferrari, Karl Kling's Mercedes, Maglioli's Ferrari and Fangio's Mercedes."

Jenkinson was the only journalist in a position to know what was happening in the winning car for the full course of the race but he, perforce, had to rely on pieces of paper thrust at him when they paused at the control points. The amazing thing was that he was capable of piecing the race together afterwards and writing it all down in his usual longhand. Even more amazing was that, when he had finished penning a most famous piece of journalistic race coverage, he put it in an envelope addressed to the offices of *Motor Sport* in London, and popped it into an Italian letter box for normal mail to the UK! The course of motor racing history could have been changed, or at least made the poorer, if that envelope had been lost in a notoriously unreliable system ...

While you might have read and re-read Jenks's amazing *Motor Sport* report of the race, you would have sympathised with the little man when he was sick over the side. "Ever since leaving the start we had had the rising sun shining in our eyes and, now, with the continual effects of sideways 'G' on my body, my poor stomach was beginning to suffer and, together with the heat from the gearbox by my left buttock, the engine fumes and the nauseating brake lining smells from the inboard-mounted brakes, it cried 'enough' and what little breakfast I had eaten went overboard, together with my spectacles, for I had made the fatal mistake of turning my head sideways at 150mph with my goggles lowered. Fortunately I had a spare pair, and there was no time to worry about a protesting stomach, for we were approaching Pesaro, where there was a sharp corner ..."

Then there was the famous flight of the Mercedes. "On one straight, lined with trees, we had marked down a hump in the road as being 'flat-out' only if the road was dry. It was, so I gave the appropriate signal and with 7,500rpm in fifth gear on the tachometer we took off, for we had made an error in our estimation of the severity of the hump. For a measurable amount of time the vibro-massage that you get sitting in a 300SLR at that speed suddenly ceased, and there was time for us to look at each other with raised eyebrows before we landed again. Even had we been in the air for only one second we should have travelled some 200 feet through the air, and I estimated the 'duration of flight' at something more than one second. The road was dead straight and the Mercedes-Benz made the perfect four-point landing and I thankfully praised the driver that he didn't move the wheel a fraction of an inch, for that would have been our end ..."

I suppose incidents like that tend to dwell on your mind. Stirling remembered the 'flight' in his splendid memoir *My Cars, My Career* written with Doug Nye. "The SLR took off like an aeroplane. I kept the steering wheel loose but straight, and after an awfully long pause as we flew through the air the wheels touched down, thankfully in line – and down went my foot again." Loose but straight ... I like that.

Getting up into the mountain passes on the homeward passage from Rome, Stirling started to suffer front brake problems. "As we climbed the Radicofani Pass one front brake began to grab, and then entering one sharp left-hander just beyond the summit it grabbed badly and caught me out. We spun to a stop, broadside with our tail in a shallow ditch, fortunately without hitting anything hard."

In fact the front brakes had simply ceased to exist, bedding metal to metal in the closing stage. In future races the 300SLRs would be fitted with four plunger pumps on the dashboard so that they could squirt oil on to any brake that grabbed! It was a quick-fix piece of engineering that cured the immediate problem for the rest of that summer.

Before the start, Fangio had given Stirling and Jenks an Argentinian stay-awake pill. Stirling took his, but Jenks kept his and gave it to Stirling's father for analysis. "There were apparently a couple of weird South American compounds involved, which the chemists were very wary of attempting to reproduce." Moss had raced all-out for just on ten hours and yet he was still chipper. After a long soak in a hot bath, followed by dinner he was still wide awake so he drove his 220A Mercedes road car back to Stuttgart for lunch with the Daimler board the next day and then home to London. I wonder what was in that pill? And would it have been just coincidence that Elvis Presley experimented with an early form of 'speed' pill in 1954 and didn't sleep for three days? Just as well they didn't do dope tests for athletes taking performance enhancing drugs in 1955!

Moss was the perfect driver for Mercedes that summer, a man who revelled in the near perfection of the machinery he was racing. "We had averaged 97.95mph for the 1,000 miles and the car's engine cover had never been raised. Back in Stuttgart the engine, when tested, gave identical power to when it had been built – 296bhp at 7,400rpm. What a testimony to Mercedes engineering..."

*Chapter 5*

# FERRARI'S MYSTERY TWIN-CYLINDER GRAND PRIX ENGINE

Michael Schumacher and Rubens Barrichello start each Grand Prix these days with full confidence in their cars but in 1955 the Ferrari team was in total disarray and, in desperation, chief designer Aurelio Lampredi designed and built a 2.5-litre *twin-cylinder* engine to try and get more torque for the tight Monaco street circuit. He would also design a more conventional in-line 2.5-litre six-cylinder for the faster tracks. It was current 1950s practice to have long-chassis and short-chassis variants of the same model to suit different circuits, but Lampredi planned two completely different cars and engines for the 1955 season, knowing that the major challenge would come from the Mercedes driven by Fangio and Moss.

His idea was to have a short, lightweight car for Monaco with an engine that produced plenty of torque since punch low-down would be more important than top-end power on such a stop-go track. The other, longer, more conventional car was for faster circuits like Reims or Spa-Francorchamps.

The Ferrari drawing office design number for the secret twin was 116F and for an engine destined never to be installed in a racing car – it tore the test bed to pieces when it was started! – it certainly excited engineering comment.

The two cylinders, with 4-valves each, had the muscular bore and stroke of 118 x 114mm giving a total capacity of 2,493cc and before the vibration tore up the dynamometer mountings, it was showing 175bhp at 4,800rpm, according to Hans Tanner in his book *The Ferrari*. Tanner merely mentioned it as one of the experiments carried out at Ferrari. In truth, it was an embarrassingly failed exercise that was probably better to ignore.

L. J. K. Setright in his tome *The Grand Prix Car 1954–1966* refers to the twin as a 'grotesque' engine but this was surely the learned Leonard's sense of engineering elegance being offended rather than the aesthetics of what is outwardly a neatly packaged power unit giving no suggestion of what lies inside.

The secret Ferrari F1 twin-cylinder was discovered only after UK Ferrari collector, Anthony Bamford, bought the Ferrari racing scrapheap behind the factory and shipped a lorry-load back to his garage. Son of J.C. Bamford, the man who established the JCB excavators company, Anthony had the finance to pursue his motoring enthusiasms. When the bits were unloaded there were around 30 engines of various shapes, sizes and vintages. There were fours, V6s, V8s and what looked like a strange little four-cylinder – which actually turned out to be the twin when cleaned up and dismantled. There were also V12s with inside and outside exhausts, some with fuel injection and some with carburettors.

Bamford's mechanic Bryan Morley had an interesting mix of engines to investigate and restore.

"When I bought the engines, Mr. Ferrari probably thought I was some sort of mad Englishman," Bamford recalled. "He told me there might be some strange engines in the load, and at first we thought the twin was some weird sort of small four. Everything was very dirty and it was hard to tell what was what. I asked him why he had this policy of scrapping everything instead of restoring cars and keeping them and he said he regretted not having kept more of his older cars, but he was an engineer and he was always thinking only of the future. They were always experimenting and throwing things away as projects were superseded."

The failure of that big twin-cylinder was down to balance problems that would plague twins until the Japanese sun rose in the motorcycle world. The two hand-span pistons rose and fell together which set up those fatal vibrations.

Back in the 1970s, I showed these photographs – the only ones ever taken – to Tyrrell designer, Derek Gardner. "The concept of the engine is extremely interesting since it was obviously intended to produce high torque at the expense of maximum horsepower. The engine is dimensionally compact and comparatively simple yet it is rugged in its construction. At maximum power it would achieve a mean piston speed comparable with that of a contemporary 250F Maserati and it would be safe to assume that an exceptionally light, compact and reliable engine producing considerable torque (but lacking ultimate horsepower) would be the ideal power unit for a circuit such as Monaco.

"Unfortunately there seems to have been a fundamental problem in the balance of the engine. Basically it is two single-cylinder engines coupled together with the power impulses situated every 360-degrees (or one impulse per revolution). Since it is impossible to completely balance a single cylinder engine, except by methods that must be considered impractical for high-speed applications, a compromise is reached in the transfer of primary out-of-balance forces by attaching a mass balance to oppose the reciprocating weight and the weight of the crank-pin. By careful tuning it is possible to obtain virtually vibrationless performance at predetermined speeds. But single cylinder engines of 1,250cc capacity running at 4,800rpm would (and presumably did) still have considerable out-of-balance force that would manifest itself in the form of low frequency vibration of high amplitude. In short, if it didn't wreck itself, it would probably have destroyed the car..."

Ironically Ferrari was to win the Monaco Grand Prix in 1955 for which the twin-cylinder engine had been specifically designed.

*Chapter 6*

# IN THE DRINK –
# THE TALE OF THE 1955
# MONACO GRAND PRIX!

Veteran BBC broadcaster, Raymond Baxter, the velvet voice before the Murray Walker generation of motor racing broadcasters, sold his archive of motor racing notes and programmes at auction and I bought his 1955 file which included the action-packed Monaco Grand Prix. His notes were almost as good as being there beside him in the commentary box.

Ferrari was on the ropes and Enzo had entered two SuperSqualo 555s for Harry Schell and Piero Taruffi and two older *Tipo* 625s for Maurice Trintignant and Nino Farina. There was no optimism in the air around the Ferrari pits.

Mercedes came confident to Monaco with new short-chassis W196s, shortened so drastically that there was no room for the inboard front brakes and these had been mounted outboard in a major engineering exercise. There were cars for Juan Manuel Fangio, Stirling Moss and Hans Herrmann. Fangio's engine had been mounted slightly further forward in the chassis, and after trying it, Moss fretted all weekend that it was better than his car.

Incredibly, the lap record round Monaco still stood to Rudolf Caracciola, set in 1937 in a supercharged 5.6-litre

Mercedes W125 at 1min 46.5sec. Paradoxically, Caracciola was refused a pit credential for the race in 1955!

The 1952 Grand Prix had been for sports cars and there were no races in 1953 and 1954. The 1955 Grand Prix was the 13th running of the race since it began in 1929.

It was fitting that Fangio, on the first day of practice, used his new Mercedes to shatter the 18-year-old Mercedes record with a pole position time of 1min 41.1sec. In a one-off ruling, the front row of the grid was set on the first day of practice! All practice laps counted for grid positions in those days – with the unique exception of this race at Monaco.

The front row was Fangio (Mercedes) with the inside running to the right-handed Gasometer Hairpin, Ascari (Lancia) and Moss (Mercedes) on the outside. In fact Ascari had equalled Fangio's pole time on the final Saturday practice session, so the race was shaping-up well.

The Mercedes dominators were not quite so dominant around the streets of the Principality. Castellotti (Lancia) and Behra (Maserati) were on row two; Mières (Maserati), Villoresi (Lancia), and Musso (Maserati) on row three; Trintignant (Ferrari) and Simon (Mercedes) on row four.

Lance Macklin in the Moss 250F Maserati and Pollet's Gordini tied for last place on the grid and they agreed to toss a coin for it, but Charles Faroux, Clerk of the Course, insisted that Pollet should start since he had set the time before Macklin, who was therefore a non-starter.

Hans Herrmann was fortunate to survive a major crash in practice when his Mercedes slammed the wall on the approach to Casino Square. He suffered a broken pelvis,

*The last hurrah. Prince Bira won the 1955 New Zealand Grand Prix in his 250F Maserati and receives the New Zealand Motor Cup from the Mayor of Auckland. It was the last victory in the distinguished career of the Siamese prince. He started racing in 1935 with a Riley Imp at Brooklands.* (LAT)

*The 1955 New Zealand Grand Prix winner, Prince Bira, in his 250F Maserati, sandwiched between the HWM-Jaguar of Lex Davison and the Ferrari of Tony Gaze. Gaze would finish third. Davison pushed over the line to claim 10th place.* (LAT)

Left: *Fangio in his Mercedes-Benz W196 during the first Grand Prix on the Buenos Aires course, run in baking heat. He won, and team-mate Stirling Moss was fourth after taking over another team car.* (David Hodges Collection)

Below: *Fangio survived heat exhaustion to win the Buenos Aires Grand Prix. At one stage in the race he pitted, exhausted, and had no idea why he had stopped. Team boss Alfred Neubauer sluiced a bucket of water over him and he continued refreshed.* (David Hodges Collection)

Right: *A fortnight later Fangio and Moss dominated the second Grand Prix on the Buenos Aires circuit, their Mercedes-Benz W196s fitted with extravagant scoops to cool the drivers after the exhaustion suffered in the previous race. They finished first and second, with Fangio ahead.* (David Hodges Collection)

Below: *Ruth Ellis and David Blakeley. Ellis was the last woman to be hanged in Britain, for the murder of Blakeley, the sometime racing driver she gunned down in cold blood outside the Magdala public house in London on Easter Sunday, 1955. (Classic & Sports Car magazine)*

*David Blakeley built and raced the Emperor-HRG sports-racing car. He was the stepson of Humphrey Cook, who funded the ERA team in the 1930s. (Classic & Sports Car magazine)*

*Stirling Moss drives Denis Jenkinson into racing history as they leave the Mille Miglia starting ramp in the Mercedes-Benz 300SLR at 7.22am, their racing number tied to their start time. (David Hodges Collection)*

*Moss guns the 300SLR Mercedes through a left-hander on the Mille Miglia. The course covered 1,000 miles of public roads closed for the race, with corners marked and padded by hay bales.* (LAT)

*Deep into the Mille Miglia and racing hard, Moss's Mercedes is distinguished by his smooth style and the Union Jack on the headrest.* (David Hodges Collection)

Above: *Moss and Jenkinson grew familiar with the 1,000-mile road course lined by eager spectators seemingly oblivious to the high speed of the 300SLR Mercedes on the rutted roads. It was a true road race!* (DaimlerChrysler Archive)

Below left: *Moss and Jenks take the chequer to win the Mille Miglia for Mercedes at record speed and write their names in racing history, averaging almost 100mph for the 1,000-mile race. The sleek Merc body was slightly dented after an argument with trackside barriers.* (David Hodges Collection)

Above: *Portly, suited Mercedes-Benz team manager Alfred Neubauer hugs his grimy new heroes after their Mille Miglia win. The bearded Jenkinson had read road notes throughout the race from his legendary 'loo roll'. Moss looks '50s race elegant in his Dunlop blue uniform with British Racing Drivers Club badge in the days before brash commercial sponsorship. British-born Mercedes engineer Rudi Uhlenhaut is on the left.* (DaimlerChrysler Archive)

Right: *The elegant Ferrari prototype 2.5-litre two-cylinder engine specially designed and built for the 1955 Monaco Grand Prix, the theory being that the superior torque would be a winner on the tight street circuit. Massive vibrational problems tore the test bed apart and the engine was never used.* (Eoin Young Archive)

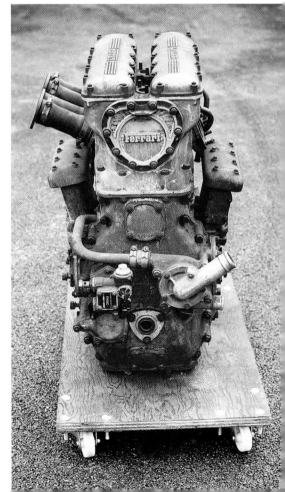

Left: *Sideview of the mystery Ferrari 2.5-litre twin. The engine eventually came to light when the canny Anthony Bamford bought the Ferrari junk yard as a job lot – and the twin-cylinder prototype was discovered!* (Eoin Young Archive)

Below: *Luck was with Ferrari at Monaco in 1955, the only Grand Prix of the season that Mercedes did not win. Maurice Trintignant was entered as a second string driver in one of the previous season's Tipo 625 Ferraris and he outlasted the pacemakers to win the first Grand Prix of his 14-year career. He would win only one more Grand Prix – also at Monaco, in 1958 driving Rob Walker's Cooper.* (David Hodges Collection)

Right: *Alberto Ascari storms up the hill to Casino Square in the D50 Lancia. He actually led the race when the Moss Mercedes stopped, but the Lancia careered into the harbour before Alberto could be told he was leading.* (David Hodges Collection)

Below: *Ascari sits snug in the cockpit of the works D50 Lancia with its distinctive pontoon-style fuel tanks. World Champion in 1952 and 1953, Ascari offered the most serious opposition to Mercedes, but Monaco would be his last race.* (David Hodges Collection)

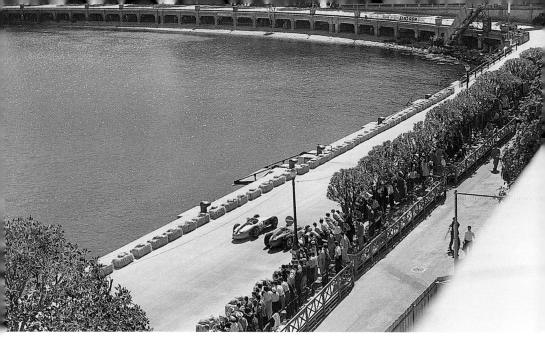

Monaco's quay-side bollards were protected by hay bales. Ascari would make history in 1955 when his Lancia plunged through the bales and into the harbour. Alberto, who had just taken the lead on that fateful lap, emerged with minor injuries but tragically he would meet his death in a mysterious accident a few days later, testing a Ferrari sports-racer at Monza. (David Hodges Collection)

Juan Manuel Fangio comfortably in the lead with the W196 Mercedes at Monaco – until an adjusting screw in the valve system broke and the engine failed. This same minor problem would eliminate all three Mercedes. (David Hodges Collection)

*Fangio has the inside running into the first turn at Monaco in 1955 with team-mate Moss powering around the outside. Ascari (26) had equalled Fangio's pole time and split the pair of Mercedes on the front row but he faltered at the start, slotting into third place. (David Hodges Collection)*

*Speedway owner Tony Hulman stands in the Chevrolet pace car leading the field away for the 1955 Indianapolis 500. Pole man was Jerry Hoyt (23), who qualified at 140.045mph on a weather-battered first day of qualification. Bill Vukovich started from the second row although he had qualified faster than the pole man at 141.071mph on the second qualifying weekend. That first qualifying day was all-important. Gary Bettenhausen (10) would finish second to Bob Sweikert in the 1955 race. (LAT)*

*Peter Ustinov hamming it up as a photographer with Graham Hill in the Monaco pits before the race in 1967. TV presenter Alan Whicker laughs (left). Ustinov was a witness to Lorenzo Bandini's fiery Ferrari crash at the chicane. His popular skit* The Grand Prix of Gibraltar *was based around the antics at the 1955 Monaco Grand Prix and has recently been made available on CD. (Geoff Goddard)*

*Cover art of Peter Ustinov posing in the engine bay of a Jaguar, for the original LP record and later used for the CD. Ustinov did all the voices and accents of drivers and team management – and the engine noises. He said he had a cold that day, which helped with the engine sounds ... Girling Moss, Jose Julio Fandango, Toby Cooks and Bill Dill were take-offs of Stirling Moss, Juan Manuel Fangio, Tony Brooks and Phil Hill.*

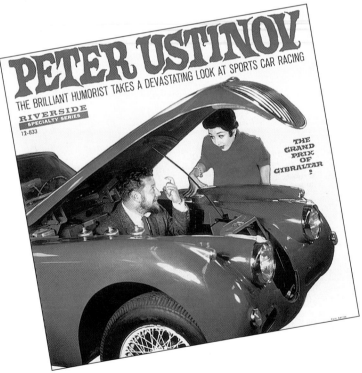

A composed Juan Manuel Fangio on his way to winning the 1955 Belgian Grand Prix at Spa in the W196 Mercedes-Benz, and taking fastest lap. (David Hodges Collection)

Johnny Lockett leads Ted Lund in the works MGA prototypes at Le Mans in 1955. These competition MGAs were identical in shape to the production versions that would be announced at Earls Court later in the year, but they had hand-beaten aluminium bodies. The race cars were fitted with four-cylinder 1.5-litre engines tuned to give 82.5bhp, compared with the 68bhp of the production cars. Alec Hounslow, who had ridden with Tazio Nuvolari in the 1932 Ards TT, was MG team manager at Le Mans. (LAT)

*Lance Macklin in the shapely Austin-Healey 100S competition model at Le Mans in 1955. It was his car that the unfortunate Pierre Levegh slammed up the back in front of the pits, triggering the disastrous accident that killed Levegh and over 80 spectators. Macklin had been a promising race driver and a good friend of Stirling Moss, but the accident at Le Mans blighted his career and the rest of his life. (Bill Piggott Collection)*

*Mike Hawthorn in the works Jaguar D-type fought for the lead with Fangio's Mercedes-Benz in the early laps at Le Mans in 1955. Fangio has activated the rear air-brake flap. It was Hawthorn's sudden swerve into the pits on the 42nd lap that was said to have caused Macklin's Austin-Healey to move across into the path of Levegh's Mercedes, but Hawthorn always denied this. He would win a grim race for Jaguar after the Mercedes-Benz team announced the withdrawal of their cars during the night, as a mark of respect. (LAT)*

*Fangio leads in the early stages of the 1955 Le Mans race, using the driver-activated hinged rear flap as a steadying aid to braking at the ends of the long fast straights. This feature was later banned after complaints that following drivers were being unsighted.* (David Hodges Collection)

*A damp and dejected Mike Hawthorn driving the works D-type to finish and win the 1955 Le Mans race.* (David Hodges Collection)

*Mercedes Benz pair with air brakes up at Le Mans in 1955. (David Hodges Collection)*

*Pierre Levegh in Mercedes-Benz 300SLR (20) was the driver who caused the biggest crash in motor racing history. In fact he had changed his name by deed poll to take the name of his famous uncle who had raced early in the century. 'Levegh' had come close to winning at Le Mans in 1952 when he raced a Talbot single-handed but the engine broke late in the race, presenting a 1–2 victory to Mercedes. It was this link that many felt had resulted in a works Mercedes drive in 1955 for the 49-year-old Frenchman. (DaimlerChrysler Archive)*

his right thigh was shattered in six places and his hip was dislocated. He dragged himself on his elbows away from the wreck, fearing fire.

That night Stirling Moss's diary notes read *Up at 9am and to Garage for a conference. Paid expenses, etc. At 2.15 practice. My best was 3rd f.t.d. 1min 43.4sec. Ascari 1min 42sec & Fangio 1min 41.4sec!* (sic) *Old record was 1min 45sec (Carrac!). The ratios are not good & are being changed. Bed at 10pm.* As an after-note, he added *Poor Hans had an accident. He has hurt his leg and ribs.*

On Friday night, Stirling had gone to bed early, writing in his diary *Up at 5am after an awful night. Only 2½-hrs sleep. In practice I tried J.F.'s car, to take a plug cut & did 1min 41.2sec! My own best was 1min 43.8sec in my car, his is better in the corners and faster. Mine was f.t.d.*

In fact Mercedes had brought four cars and after Herrmann's crash, legendary team manager Alfred Neubauer, persuaded André Simon, if persuasion was needed, to park his private Maserati and drive the spare Mercedes.

Moss's Saturday diary included *Lunch at Salon Prive & met Bella Darvi, star of "Racers". Later saw the film & food & bed at 12.15pm.*

Stirling fails to record the story recounted by Chris Nixon in his book *The Rivals* where Moss had waved to a pretty girl at the Station Hairpin each lap of practice, signalling that they should meet up. Stirling took her to the Ali Baba Club and after a dance, they returned to their table to find a note which read *Der Moss must in der bed be, mitout meinfrau. Neubauer.* Stirling realised that the handwriting was not that of his tyrannical Mercedes team manager, and spotted Denis Jenkinson grinning in the background. Jenks had partnered Moss on the Mille Miglia the previous weekend!

Interesting that Moss noted he had been to see *Racers* (also titled *Such Men are Dangerous*) – as Kevin Desmond notes in his book *The Man with Two Shadows* – with a group of drivers including Fangio and Ascari. They went to the cinema and then for a stroll round the circuit. It was hardly likely that an Argentinian and an Italian would be going to a French movie in Monaco, so it must have been the preview of *Racers* that Stirling had attended. When they got to the chicane, Desmond noted that one of the drivers said "Whoever touches here, goes into the water" and Ascari immediately searched for something wooden to touch.

Ascari was the prisoner of superstition and the number eight loomed large in his mind-set. His father, Antonio Ascari, had been killed in a P2 Alfa Romeo bearing the number 26 $(2+6 = 8)$ during the 1925 French Grand Prix on July 26th. At Monaco in 1955, Alberto Ascari was on the front row in Lancia number 26 between the works Mercedes of Fangio and Moss which were numbered two and six equalling eight if you were into numerology. Quirky, or what? Would it have escaped Ascari's manic attention that his father was 13,463 days old when he was killed at Montlhéry? When the Monaco Grand Prix started, Alberto had been alive for 13,462 days ...

Fangio led away but Castellotti, coming fast off the second row, passed him up the hill. Fangio was soon in command again, however, leaving Castellotti to argue second place with Moss. Then Jean Behra in the Maserati was coming through to mix it with the Lancias.

It was the first race of the 1955 World Championship on the most prestigious circuit. The Mercedes train was in motion with Fangio leading and Moss in second but Simon's Mercedes had already stopped with an engine problem.

Behra was a determined third until half distance when his Maserati went off song. In his book *The Chequered Flag*, an unsung tour of the 1955 season, Douglas Rutherford wrote "The big Maserati flag went out to stop young Perdisa, circulating hopefully in sixth place. He came in, braking hard, stared in amazement at the pit staff and Behra gesticulating for him to get out of that cockpit quick. Orders is orders. Perdisa jumped out, Behra jumped into the thrashed Maserati, pulled his goggles down and drove away to do the best he could with it. But the Monaco Gremlin liked young Perdisa. It was he and not Behra who figured when the final results came out."

Ascari had moved into third place ahead of his argumentative young team-mates and the race settled down. Fangio had set fastest lap of the race and was signalled by Neubauer to ease back.

At 40 laps Raymond Baxter in the commentary booth noted in his longhand that the running order was Fangio (Mercedes), Moss (Mercedes), Behra (Maserati), Ascari (Lancia), Trintignant (Ferrari), Mières (Maserati) and Perdisa (Maserati).

On the 50th lap – half distance – Fangio was parked. Rutherford wrote that when Fangio selected second gear down into Mirabeau, the transmission failed. Was this early PR preciousness where the engines never failed, but always the accessories? Later historians, more interested in fact not fogged by race day fictions, noted that a small screw in the valve gear had failed on Fangio's Mercedes, as it had earlier on Simon's car. Both were out with engine failure and it was stalking Moss in the surviving Mercedes.

Stirling was now handily in the lead for what would be his first *Grand Épreuve* win just a week after he had wowed the motor racing world, winning the Mille Miglia for Mercedes at an average speed only just short of 100mph. Ascari was now second but far behind. Trintignant was a distant third in his old Ferrari.

Baxter's notes read *80th Lap. Moss into pits on fire and Ascari missing*. Shortly after he had crossed-out the word *missing* and over-written *in drink at chicane*. Ascari's ducking would change the face of motor racing history.

Moss, now Sir Stirling, remembers that the same minor problem had wrecked the advanced desmodromic valve system on all three Mercedes. An adjusting screw in the valve gear had broken, jammed under the camshaft and punched a hole in the cambox which gushed out oil onto the exhausts. He was not on fire, as Baxter had noted but had trailed smoke all the way from the tunnel, along the quay front, and down to the pits. He had also, inevitably, dropped oil.

"If it had been now, I would have won," said Moss at Goodwood in 2002. Why did he say that? "The race then was 100 laps – now it's down to 80 laps ..." Nixon noted that the triple failure had only happened twice before in Mercedes racing history – at Montlhéry in 1934 and Reims in 1939.

Moss had been closing on Ascari's second-placed Lancia to lap him with only 20 laps left, but the third Mercedes blow-up meant that Alberto was now in the lead on the road as he roared through Casino Square while Moss was parked at the pits. Ascari was not to know he was leading because he never got as far as the pits to get the 'P1' signal from his crew. As he came out of the tunnel and down to the jink of the chicane, the Lancia cut loose. Did something break or did he hit oil trailed from Moss's engine failure? The crowd knew from the commentator that Moss's retirement meant Ascari was leading and they were waving and cheering. Did this distract him, exhausted so late into the race as it would do 12 years later with Lorenzo Bandini in the Ferrari? Whatever the reason, he lost control, slammed the very part of the outer palisade that the drivers had joked about the night before after the movie, and somersaulted over the barrier into the harbour.

It was as well that the Lancia had a commodious cockpit and he could escape easily under water. Rutherford: "People were shouting 'there he is!' as a blue helmet bobbed to the surface and Ascari's streaked face was seen underneath it. Alberto tore off the helmet, but still holding it, he struck out with a strong over-arm, until divers had reached him and pulled him aboard their rescue boat."

So Maurice Trintignant, a veteran at 38, in a Ferrari that had been rescued from Enzo's scrap yard and dusted off, won the Grand Prix from young guns Castellotti in the Lancia and Perdisa in the 250F Maserati that Behra thought he had used up.

'Trint' could scarcely have entertained thoughts of attending the prize-giving at the palace that evening, starting in the pensionable Ferrari from 10th place on the grid. In fact he went to the palace in the lead for the 1955 World Championship! I always wondered at his French nickname *Petoulet*. He was one of four racing brothers and one, Louis was killed in his 2.3-litre supercharged Bugatti in 1933 when a gendarme wandered across the track in front of him. Five years later Maurice bought the same car back and began his own racing career which would be interrupted by war. The first post-war race in France – in Europe – was held on the Bois de Boulogne in Paris but 'Trint' was an early retirement in the gallant old Bugatti. Race winner Jean-Pierre Wimille asked after the race why he had retired and Maurice explained that the car had been stored in a barn during the war, and his fuel system had clogged with bits of straw…and *le petoulet*…rat droppings. Wimille hooted and from that day 'Trint' was known as *Petoulet*. Reliability was the most important word in Trintignant's career arsenal and he would win at Monaco again in 1958 driving Rob Walker's Cooper.

Maurice became mayor of his local village in France, close to the source of Perrier water, and established a 150-acre vineyard which produced 400,000 bottles of red and rosé each year. His favourite wine is named *Le Petoulet* with a label featuring a racing car on a chequered flag background. His delivery vans bore the slogan *Le Champion des Vins – Le Vin du Champion.*

That night after the race at Monaco, Ascari's Lancia was located in eight metres of water in the Bay of Hercules, hauled out by a crane, loaded on a trailer, and taken back to Lancia's headquarters at Turin. Ascari was bruised and suffering shock, with a painful nose and was kept in hospital overnight.

Moss wrote in his diary that night: *Up at 10am. Mucked around. Light lunch and then the race. Start at 2.45. I took the lead & waved J.F. past then Castalotti* (sic) *nipped by (half tank of gas). I repassed & from then on Fangio 1st, S.M. 2nd & we gained +30secs. Fangio then broke & I lead* (sic) *until the 81st lap, when I broke whilst 1min 38sec ahead of Ascari who went into the harbour! O.K. Later called at the hospital, saw Hans & Alberto & then reception at Casino. Bed at 3am.*

*Chapter 7*

# WORLD CHAMPION ALBERTO ASCARI KILLED

Before the Monaco GP, Ascari had obtained permission from Lancia to share a new Ferrari 750 Monza sports car with Lancia team-mate Eugenio Castellotti in the *Supercortemaggiore* 1,000-kilometre sports car race at Monza the following weekend. The car was still unpainted, running in raw aluminium.

Still resting from his high-speed Monaco ducking, Ascari took a call from Castellotti inviting him to come to Monza to watch his test laps with the new car. Alberto told his wife he would be back for lunch. It was the 26th of the month. His least favourite date. At the track he spoke with his friend Gianni Lurani, saying that he thought it was always best to get back behind the wheel as soon as possible after a crash and he asked Castellotti if he could do a few laps.

Ascari was stretching his own superstitions. He would *never* drive without his blue helmet or his blue three-button sports shirt, but now he was borrowing Castellotti's white helmet because his own was having a new chin-strap fitted after his accident. He was driving in a collar and tie. Those who knew of Ascari's deep-felt superstitions, were astonished. He had done two laps, building up speed, getting back into the feel of it and then he set off on a third lap, going for it. He was going into the Vialone curve, later to be renamed Ascari, when it happened.

Kevin Desmond, author of Ascari's biography *The Man with Two Shadows*, wrote: "Those waiting for him to complete the lap heard repeated changes of gear, then seconds later, the engine roar suddenly stopped. There was an ominous 'clank-clank-clank' then silence. Then a man came running up the track, waving his arms and looking terribly distressed."

The Ferrari had spun, somersaulted and thrown Ascari out. He lay on his back, unconscious, Castellotti's borrowed white helmet split in two. He died of massive injuries on his way to hospital by ambulance.

All Italy went into mourning. La Scala closed on the evening of his funeral as a mark of national respect.

As with all accidents involving top drivers in mysterious circumstances, there was a variety of reasons put forward: that he had blacked-out as a delayed result of his Monaco crash, that he had missed a gearshift, or that a workman was crossing the track and Ascari had lost control trying to avoid him … but Mike Hawthorn had his own theory which seemed to make more sense.

Mike was sharing a 750 Monza Ferrari with Umberto Maglioli in the race and had arrived at the track about an hour after Ascari's crash. They had been unable to get 6.50 x 16 tyres for the race and had to use 7.00 x 16 tyres. Hawthorn said he had tried their car on these tyres and in his first biography *Challenge Me the Race* he wrote "I found it very nasty indeed when it came to the Vialone Curve,

89

where there were a lot of little ripples on the road surface. I came to the conclusion that the rims were too narrow for these tyres and had them taken off my car. Where Ascari crashed there were long, broad, black tyre marks, followed by marks of the wheel rims digging into the road, and it seemed to me that he probably changed into fifth just as he hit the ripples, the car started to slide, the tyres rolled under and the rims gouged into the road, causing it to somersault ..."

As recounted in the Monaco chapter, Alberto was obsessed with superstition and the importance of numbers – called *cabella* in Italian. His father, Antonio, was killed while leading the GP of France on July 26th, 1925, at the age of 36, four days after a serious accident. Alberto, 30 years later, also 36 years old, was killed on May 26th, only four days after receiving a strong warning from destiny at Monaco, where he drove Lancia No 26.

Ascari was seven when his father was killed and this may have had a bearing on his tough treatment of his own son, as a racer's way of shielding the boy from too much affection in case the same thing happened to him and he never came home.

Alberto started racing Bianchi motorcycles in 1937 when he was 19 and three years later Enzo Ferrari signed him to drive the new *Tipo* 815 two-seater eight-cylinder 1.5-litre sports car in the Mille Miglia. It made history as the first Ferrari to race, because Enzo was bound by his Alfa Romeo agreement not to build cars under his own name, hence the prototype racing as a type number and not a name. Alberto shared the car with his cousin, Minozzi, who was an experienced Alfa Romeo racer. The new car dominated the race in the opening stages but it was out with valve failure after 90 miles.

With the war over, Ascari's next showing was in the Cisitalia (CIS-Italia) 'road show' of 16 drivers, the idea being to offer a ready-made race to promoters. The Cisitalia company was backed by a financial conglomerate: 'Conzorzio Industriale Sportive Italia'. The first – and only – appearance of the one-make 16-driver squad that included Chiron, Lurani, Brivio, Taruffi and the young Ascari, was in Egypt on a course near Cairo in 1947. Alberto finished second to Taruffi in his heat and second to Cortese in the final, a performance which earned him a drive with Scuderia Ambrosiana as number two to the experienced Luigi Villoresi who would become his mentor and close friend. It was Ascari who debuted the Maserati 16-valve supercharged 4CLT (T for *tubulari* chassis) at Reims in 1947 but his only win was at the wheel of a Maserati A6GC sports-racer in the Circuit of Modena.

The 1948 season started with a win in the revised 4CLT/48 Maserati at San Remo, and the car became known as the San Remo Maserati. Villoresi had been second. They were 1–2 again in the Circuit of Modena. And in the British Grand Prix at Silverstone, Alberto was second to Villoresi in another team 1–2. The Alfa Romeo team management was well aware of the young Ascari following in his father's wheel-tracks, and with a touch of history they offered him a drive in a *Tipo* 158 works car in the 1948 French Grand Prix at Reims where he finished third behind team-mates Wimille and Sanesi.

The 1949 season started with a win in his Ambrosiana Maserati in the Buenos Aires Grand Prix. Enzo Ferrari re-entered the Ascari family story when he signed Alberto and Luigi to drive Ferraris and the die was cast. They won Formula 1 and Formula 2 races all over Europe. In 1950 he won nine races and in 1951 he was six times a winner, but in 1952 he won twelve races in the tidy little 2-litre Ferrari 500 and became World Champion in a season when all the *grandes épreuves* were for Formula 2.

In 1952 Ascari was away on a new adventure with a special version of the *Tipo* 375 4.5-litre V12 Ferrari Grand Prix car of the old formula, fitted out for the 500-mile race at Indianapolis. The Americans were suitably impressed with the high-tech Ferrari compared with their simpler, strapping Offenhauser-powered cars, but Ascari was sidelined when a wire wheel collapsed.

It was *déjà vu* for Alberto in 1953 when he won the GPs in Argentina, Holland, Belgium, Britain, Germany and Switzerland to take his second world title on the trot in dominant style.

The new Lancia team appeared in some style for 1954, signing Ascari and Villoresi before the cars were ready to race. So Alberto appeared for Maserati and Ferrari during the summer, racing the new Lancia D50 only once, retiring with clutch failure in the Spanish GP on the Pedralbes circuit. High point in an otherwise gloomy summer was a fine win for Lancia in the Mille Miglia.

The Lancia D50s, with their distinctive pontoon tanks slung between the wheels either side of the car, found form in 1955 and it seemed that Alberto was going to be able to take the fight to the new Mercedes W196 cars driven by Fangio and Moss. He led in Argentina, besting the Mercedes, but spun on melting tar and abandoned. He would win the non-title GPs in Turin and Naples, races not on the Mercedes schedule, and for the Monaco Grand Prix he would equal Fangio's pole position lap time.

The rest is history...

*Chapter 8*

# FATAL HAT-TRICK
# AT INDY

But for a snapped pin in the steering arm ten laps from the finish of the 1952 Indianapolis 500, Bill Vukovich could have been going for a record-breaking, history-making fourth Indy win in succession when the man said "Gentleman…start your engines…!" in 1955. He had won the '500' in 1953 and 1954 and now he was aiming at an unprecedented three-in-a-row at the Speedway. Other drivers had won the 500 three times – Lou Meyer, Wilbur Shaw and Mauri Rose – but none had won three times in succession. Vukie was aiming for the big one. The hat-trick.

Indianapolis thrives on tradition. After the drum majorettes from the Purdue University Band did their traditional high kicks in skimpy skirts on that chilly morning, the players in the band were arranged on the track to form the name 'Shaw' as a mark of respect. Three-time winner Wilbur had been killed in an air crash the previous October.

Vukie – 'The Fresno Flyer' – was born William Vucerovitch in Alameda, California, in 1919. He learned engineering the hard way, maintaining army trucks and jeeps during World War Two, and eventually put together enough cash to buy a midget racer, which he painted red and named 'Old Ironsides', in those hectic post-war years in California. He won the West Coast title in 1946 and 1947 and in 1950 he was national champion.

Vukovich regarded racing purely as a means of making money. Dollars won on the track had financed his service station in Fresno, California. He planned others. He had come up through the dirt tracks and now he was determined to concentrate on where the money was – Indianapolis. Indy was his ultimate speed plant, two and a half miles of pure beauty and speed with payoffs to match. Vukie seemed to feel that Indianapolis was his own personal playground. And after discovering the speed 'Mecca' he decided it didn't make much financial sense to compete in other events on the championship trail for the risks involved. People were losing their lives in other races and while Indy was dangerous it was still only one race a year for four and a half hours. Surely he could survive. Surely he would succeed.

The Indianapolis Motor Speedway is the way it was and the famous 500-mile is the way it is when the track first opened in 1909, because the two and a half mile rectangular circuit was the maximum configuration in the plot of land that Carl Fisher had bought for his motor track. The race was to be 500 miles because that was the maximum distance that could then be run in daylight hours.

It is a sobering thought that the lap record in 1955 was 144mph and fifty years later the record around that same rectangular circuit, same 2.5-miles, same walls, was nearly 100mph faster. In 1955, Grand Prix technology had yet to arrive at the Brickyard and the front-engined roadsters were supreme. In fact post-war Grand Prix technology had been to the Brickyard in 1952 when Alberto Ascari arrived with a track version of the *Tipo* 375 4.5-litre Grand Prix Ferrari. It was out-paced, out of its depth in a different bowl, and Ascari was out with a collapsed wheel. Ferrari never went back. Grand Prix technology came with Cooper and Jack Brabham in 1961 and then Lotus and Jim Clark in 1963 but the speed hike really arrived with the orange McLaren-Offenhauser 'wedge' M16 in 1971.

Until 1960 a win in the Indianapolis 500 counted for the Formula 1 World Championship, so the quaint result was that in 1953 Bill Vukovich appeared seventh in the championship results (behind Ascari, Fangio, Farina, Hawthorn, Villoresi and Gonzalez) with nine points – eight for a win and one for fastest lap. In 1954 he was sixth equal on eight points with Mercedes rookie driver, Hans Herrmann, who collected one point for fastest lap in France, four points for third in the Swiss GP and three points for fourth place in Italy.

Visit the Hopkins garage on the eve of the 1955 '500' where Vukovich's team mechanics Jim Travers and Frank Coon were preparing the car. This pair of perfectionists would form Traco Engineering and fettle the first Oldsmobile V8 engines for Bruce McLaren's sports cars that grew into CanAm dominators. "I spent several hours the night before the race talking to the crew and looking over this handsome, low-slung beast, finished in metallic blue with startling red upholstery," wrote John Bentley in *The Autocar*. I wonder what that dry pair, Travers and Coon, who had always looked after Vukie's cars, thought of having a journalist wanting to 'talk for several hours' the night before the race. "Everything had been magnafluxed twice – before and after qualification; every nut was safety-wired; a brand new crankshaft had just been installed as a routine precautionary measure. You could have eaten off the spotless, gleaming 'Offy' engine, off-set and canted at 38° for better weight distribution and lower frontal area. Lovingly they drained the petrol tank so as not to impose unnecessary overnight loads on the critical torsion bar setting."

Bentley described Vukovich as an enigmatic fellow. "He was sallow, snappy-eyed, yet with a dead-pan countenance that masked an irresistible determination. A Scrooge with words among strangers, but always ready with an amusing quip for those he knew. We asked him how he rated his chances with the new machine. 'Makes no difference what you win it in,' he said. 'All these cars turn left. If you turn right, that's when you're in trouble.'"

A wealthy Californian sportsman, Howard Keck, had sponsored Vukovich's car when he won in 1953 and 1954 and the story went that when Vukie won in 1954 Keck was on the 14th hole of a golf course when someone told him his car had just won the Indy 500. It was reported that Keck was actually quite annoyed because he had bought the racing car as a tax write-off and the race win had bumped him into a higher tax bracket. Not at all what he needed, and he withdrew his backing for Vukie at the end of the season. Sponsorship of car and crew was taken up by Lindsey Hopkins for 1955.

High winds on the all-important first day of qualifying at the speedway kept cars off the track but with half an hour to go before the 6pm cut-off, Jerry Hoyt went out in the Jim Robbins Special and racked up a four-lap average of 140.045mph on a blustery track. Only one other driver – Tony Bettenhausen – braved a qualifying run in the time available but he couldn't better Hoyt, who was announced as pole sitter, regardless of what times and speeds were set on the three subsequent qualifying days.

The following day Vukovich qualified at 141.071mph for third fastest time that Sunday so that he would start fifth fastest on the second row, behind the two faster Sunday qualifiers – Fred Agabashian and Jack McGrath – and the only two cars that had qualified on the opening day. Hoyt was on pole at 140.045mph and Vukie was back on row two at the faster time of 141.071mph because of the age-old qualifying rules.

Race day was cold and windy. Flags whipped sharply from their poles around the track. McGrath took the lead from the start, Vukie was in front on the fourth lap and they battled back and forth over the opening laps until Vukovich started to pull away after 28 laps. After 125 miles Vukie had a 20sec lead on McGrath, set a new 50-lap record at 136.212mph and was passing and lapping the seventh-place man. There were reports that the wind was moving the cars on the straights. McGrath was out with magneto problems and Vukie's hat-trick was looking good ... until Roger Ward's car (Ruttman's winning machine from 1952) snapped an axle and went out of control as Vukovich was coming up to lap the three-car group of Ward, Keller and Boyd. Descriptions of what happened next vary but the end result did not change. Bill Vukovich perished with a fractured skull, trapped beneath his blazing car.

In his book *500 Miles to Go*, Al Bloemaker, public relations director at the Speedway, wrote "Keller swerved to the left instinctively avoiding Ward's car, and found himself headed straight for a concrete abutment which supported a golfer's footbridge over the racing strip. In a desperate effort to avoid disaster, he cut his wheels to the right, sideswiped Boyd's car, and knocked it directly into Vukie's path as the 1953–54 winner headed for a six-foot opening between Ward's overturned car and the outer wall.

"The left front wheel of Vukie's car went up and over the right rear wheel of Boyd's car. Boyd's car did a barrel roll. Vukie's airborne, cleared the barrier without touching it, did a complete roll in the air, and hit the ground nose first. On the first bounce it reached a height of 35 feet, spinning end over end. Then it bounced sickeningly a second time and crashed in flames, upside down, with Vukie – already dead of a skull fracture – pinned in the cockpit."

Sitting high in the Press Box overlooking the pits, John Bentley wrote in *The Autocar* "I saw the sudden cruel pillar of smoke drifting skywards on the back stretch, bare seconds after the yellow caution light came on. Directly opposite, with his name neatly painted on the whitewashed pit wall, was Vukovich's pit. The blaring, cacophonous public address system, always laggard and vague in announcing accidents, was silent for an interminable time as the brightly-hued machines, garlanded round the course, maintained positions at reduced speed with subdued growls. No 4 was long overdue and at first Vukovich's devoted crew peered wonderingly up the straightaway. Then someone must have brought the news by telephone. The expressions of those men were unforgettable. For one paralysing instant they stood there looking like small boys, utterly bewildered by a sudden thrashing for something they hadn't done. And then they were gone..."

Bob Sweikert went on to win the race.

Vukovich's death spawned the theories and questions that mirror President Kennedy's assassination. Investigators have gone to great lengths to trace original photographs, film and reports of the crash. One report read "According to photographic evidence and eyewitness accounts, three vehicles outside the fence were damaged – a blue and white Studebaker 4-door sedan, a red Ford F100 pickup truck and a white Speedway Safety Patrol Jeep. The exact involvement of these vehicles is one of the most important factors in determining exactly what inflicted the injuries to Vukovich in the accident. A very important photo shows the Studebaker sedan and the Ford F-100 pickup parked side by side, both with serious damage to their hoods (bonnets). In fact the Ford pickup was smashed so severely that the radiator was ruptured and was leaking water. The Jeep had damage to its windshield, cloth top, steering wheel and steering column. When looking at movies and comparing them to the damage to the vehicles and their respective locations it can be difficult to see how the Vukovich car in its travel could have caused the damage to the Jeep but it wasn't impossible. It is also difficult to see how the tyre could have caused the damage as well. After exhaustive examination it was determined that the damage to the sedan and the pickup was so severe and of such a nature that a tyre could not have done it. It had to have been Vukovich's car, that much is certain..."

It was questioned whether Ward's car had broken an axle. The car was too badly damaged for certainty. One theory was that it might have been a gusting wind that flicked him into the wall.

Ed Elisian, one of Vukie's small circle of close friends, stopped his car and ran to try and help. He said in a newspaper interview "I came out of the corner and saw the other cars and knowing Vukie had just passed me I knew it was he who went over the wall and that the car was on fire. I immediately braked my car and went into the infield, jumped out and ran over to help my friend Billy." Safety crews had to stop Elisian from trying to overturn Vukovich's burning car, for his own safety. One report suggested that Elisian's car owner was furious that he had stopped, but his gesture won him an award for his sportsmanship. That Elisian was in the race at all was the subject of comment during qualifying. When it appeared that he would not get a chance to qualify on the rain-delayed final day, he offered $100 to a driver close to the head of the queue to take his place. He went out with ten minutes to go but there was confusion on flagging for his qualifying run and he was rejected. Angry protests followed, the timing tapes were re-checked, and in an unheard of move, Elisian was allowed out for another four lap run at 7pm – an hour after the final closure of qualifying!

It was Ward hitting the wall that triggered the fatal high-speed chain of events and when he was interviewed the next day he said "I was coming out of the southeast turn when the wind got me." A later investigative report said "The car (Ward's) did spin in a way which was indicative of being hit by a gust of wind, as the tail came around in an unusual fashion to the left, almost as though he was trying to correct from a gust of wind. If it had been oil on the track, the car should have gone loose and spun the other way. As regards a broken axle, there has never been any mention as to which axle could have broken. In one aftermath photo there is evidence of a broken axle with both left front and left rear wheels askew. But since the car rolled over two times this damage could easily have been done in the accident. In another indication that the wind was severe enough to cause a driver to lose control, Tony Bettenhausen (one of the two who had qualified on the first day) said after the race that the wind was worse than when he qualified. Race winner Bob Sweikert said that the wind had been so bad that 'it was making the cars move around six feet...'"

*Chapter 9*

# GRAND PRIX
# DU ROC

Peter Ustinov was the ultimate actor enthusiast, an artiste who could absorb a subject and project it at will. In 1955 he was a keen follower of motor sport and was at Monaco for the Grand Prix, watching from a viewpoint above the chicane where the cars came storming out of the tunnel's mouth into the sunlight, braking down into the double corner, swinging left and then right and then accelerating hard down to the seafront to the left-hander at *Bureau Tabac* where a long established tobacconist's kiosk had given its name forever to a corner on the famous circuit. He actually witnessed Alberto Ascari smashing through the barriers at the chicane and splashing into the high-dollar harbour.

Sir Peter Ustinov, who died in his 80s as this book was in production, was the star of 90 movies and director and producer of many more. He was knighted in 1990.

In 2002, Ace Records, the London company who had bought the rights to Riverside Records, a Californian specialist company that produced long-playing records of motor racing and racing car sounds in the 1950s, asked Nigel Roebuck, specialist F1 columnist for *Autosport* and a journalist with a special feel for the 'fifties, if he would track down Sir Peter Ustinov and interview him for sleeve notes to accompany their copy of *The Grand Prix of Gibraltar* now transferred to compact disc.

Roebuck traced Ustinov to New York and did his interview by telephone, at first diffident, worried at his chances of finding the ageing film star in any mood to reminisce on something he had done nearly half a century before. "It was a long time ago now, a single day in a long and extraordinarily varied career, but Sir Peter remembered *The Grand Prix of Gibraltar* with affection and pride." It was a huge hit in the motor racing world, taking off all the personalities, mimicking the accents of the different drivers and team managers. It became an instant cult item. If you couldn't quote from it at length and remember all the nicknames, you became suspect, not a true believer.

"The thing is," Sir Peter told Roebuck, "I was very interested in motor racing and therefore knew more about it than many people would imagine. I knew some of the personalities involved, like Stirling." Those were the days when celebrity enthusiasts mingled in the pits, unheralded, invited as a mate of someone's, rather than the hyped 'star guests' seen in the Grand Prix paddock and pitlane today. "The only melancholy thing is how many of them aren't here any more, like Wolfgang von Trips – von Grips on the record – who was an awfully nice man and very un-Germanic. In fact, he was one of those Germans who spoke English rather too well to be true: 'You know, we're all going over for the weekend after next, *unt*, er, we shall enjoy ourselves.'"

Roebuck observed that Sir Peter had difficulty in imagining a similarly satiric piece about the sport today.

He remembered that he had a bad cold when he made the original recording and reckons that was no bad thing. "In fact it helped very much with the sound of the Ferraris – for some reason a cold seems to help you simulate 12 cylinders! Normally you can only do eight ..." When he walked into that studio in Manhattan that day Sir Peter had little idea he was about to make a record for the ages, with a cult following as strong now as when it was released. "I was very interested in motor racing at that time – still am in fact, although I don't go to the Grands Prix any more. And there was this strange company called Riverside Records, which specialised mainly in jazz, as far as I remember, but also produced a number of records of racing engine noises – there must have been some very perverse people around at the time, buying records so they could sit at home and listen to revving engines, but there it was!"

In fact Riverside also produced a series of LP records capturing live recordings of interviews on 33⅓rpm vinyl with the likes of the Marquis de Portago, Carroll Shelby, Phil Hill and Stirling Moss.

"Anyway, the Riverside people had the idea of my trying something, a sort of satirical record about motor racing and in order to tempt me they gave me a selection of records of Alfa Romeos farting, and so on! Quite honestly, I never really played them because the sound was so unattractive out of its context – without the *smell* and so on. But anyway, I agreed. They had no idea what I was going to do – and I, frankly, had no idea, either ..."

What emerged, wrote Roebuck, was a gem of universal comedy. While at one level a devotee of motor racing can savour Ustinov's obvious love of the sport and affectionate 'insider' jokes, so also *The Grand Prix of Gibraltar* is easily appreciated by anyone who takes pleasure simply in the quirks of human nature and differing nationalities in a funny tale sublimely told.

There is the manager of the German Schnorcedes team for example, Herr Altbauer (a take-off on Mercedes team manager, Neubauer) who has thought everything through in the minutest detail, who runs his team like a military operation. Wagner is played in the pits continuously, and the drivers are required to blow their noses seven and a half minutes before the start, laboratory investigations having revealed that this is the best time to ensure the nose is completely clear for the race. "This is important," says Altbauer, "because a handkerchief carried in the pocket would be extra weight! As we have no central pocket on our overalls, a handkerchief would have to be either in the left pocket or in the right pocket – which would completely destroy the balance of this revolutionary new car which we have adopted..." He finishes the pre-race interview thus: "I would ask you not to ask any more questions. There will be a formal press release after our victory."

Ustinov had drawn on Alfred Neubauer, the legendary team manager of Mercedes. "In fact," he remembered "I had to give Neubauer a copy of the record as a present. He listened to it glumly, and said 'It's very kind of you – but I don't see what's funny'. Which I thought made my point very well..."

Neubauer thought it had been a documentary.

In the next pit we find Orgini, the French team, and a counterpoint in every respect to Altbauer and Schnorcedes. "I separated 'the cast' into groups in my mind," says Ustinov, "and so we had the French who never had enough money even to clean their cars, who had girls everywhere, who brought inflammable liquids into their pits, yet smoked constantly: 'Oh, it's all right – the cars are insured ...' The model for Orgini was Amédée Gordini, who ran a perennially under-funded Grand Prix team in the 1950s. "I knew him, and he was absolutely the prototype of that kind of Frenchman ... rather dirty hands, with oil encrusted in them, a cigarette in his mouth the whole time ..."

Ferrari may be a model of discipline and orderliness in the Michael Schumacher era of today, but it wasn't always so, and Ustinov's Fanfani team reflects to perfection the Latin chaos of a time gone by. "Commendatore Fanfani, have you got a moment?" Asks the commentator. "I have all the time in the world, since I am retiring from racing," snaps Fanfani, and again Ustinov is borrowing from reality: time was when the irascible Commendatore Enzo Ferrari was always threatening to withdraw his cars from competition.

Fanfani's number one driver is José Julio Fandango (Juan Manuel Fangio), and he faces competition from, among others, the British Pinfall (Vanwall) team, whose drivers are Girling Foss (Stirling Moss) and Toby Cooks (Tony Brooks), and the lone American Wildfowl driven by Bill Dill (Phil Hill). "I can't remember where the name 'Wildfowl' came from," says Ustinov, "but I think it probably had something to do with the Americans' rather romantic view of these things – even if they call their aeroplanes 'Thundercloud' and rubbish like that! 'Wildfowl' seemed like a name that had been missed by others ..." It was not, however, an ideal vehicle for the tortuous track on Gibraltar. "The power steering," says Bill Dill, "makes it practically impossible to turn at less than 90 degrees – that presents its own special problems. We're trying to lighten it as much as possible, by taking out the ashtrays, and substituting a smaller dash clock. And if there's time – and I don't know if there is – we're going to ditch the armrests." The commentator observes that there is a lot of chrome on the car. "Yes," says Dill, "the weight of the chrome alone is more than the entire Schnorcedes..."

Guest of Honour at the race is to be the Duke of Edinburgh, who will drive a lap of the circuit in his de-tuned Morris, but his arrival is delayed and at the drivers' meeting, the Chief Steward advises competitors of the appropriate protocol. "If His Royal Highness should arrive during the race, of course the race will stop until he has taken his place in his box. Stop your cars and rise in the driver's seat until given the signal to proceed once more."

Predictably, mayhem ensues. The race is started by the Governor of Gibraltar, Lord Weeps of Sebring. "The Governor's dropped the flag!" exclaims the British commentator, Roland Thaxter (Raymond Baxter). "That is, the Governor dropped, and he carried the flag down with him..." "Lord Weeps was so old that he couldn't really remember a sentence," says Ustinov. "I got that idea from [General] Montgomery, who once said, 'There are four cardinal points: education, discipline – and courage'."

Sir Peter's gift for mimicry was surely never better heard than on this recording. Quite apart from all the different voices, the innumerable accents, he contributes the engine sounds, the marching feet of a regiment of the

Royal Fusiliers, the band's playing of 'Land of Hope and Glory', even the klaxon warning of the race's imminent start, "The record company came in afterwards," says Ustinov, "with a few noises that are really impossible to do, like a hammer against a piece of metal. They sort of burnished it, after it was finished. But everything else was me – even the window being opened in the drivers' meeting!"

Everything fits together so seamlessly that it is even more astonishing when Ustinov told Roebuck that he had no prepared script when he arrived at the studio in New York. "We had to record it there, because I was appearing in my play *Romanoff and Juliet* on Broadway at the time, and because it was very difficult to think clearly about anything else, I did *Grand Prix of Gibraltar* very quickly. It wasn't scripted at all – the whole thing was improvised, and done in one day. I remember later having to go to another studio and climb inside a very oily Jaguar for the cover photograph, and that was that. I made a few notes before the recording, working out the drivers' and teams' names, and so on, but that was all. In fact it had a sort of shape in mind, because a race has a definite shape: they've got to practise and then they've got to start, and they've got to finish. The Governor has to make his speech and eventually fall down – presumably dead! – in order to start the race, and everything was underway. I didn't write a script because I'm much better without one in circumstances like that. It's really like thinking aloud – I mean, what is a script except what you put down when you think of it? I've always been rather keen on improvisation. The Riverside people didn't really know what they'd got until they put it together. Then, rather too late to help them, unfortunately, it became a sort of cult thing. They themselves went bust. I chose Gibraltar because it's an ideal place for an absurd motor race. I mean, once you've got Monaco, you might as well have Gibraltar! It's pleasantly absurd – the track going up the rock face, and coming down the other side, through pedestrian zones, and so on. No passing on the cliff face, of course, that's fairly obvious ... Gibraltar has a very strange aroma to it, I've found. I once went to a shop there, where a very genial red-haired Jewish gentleman had four suits ready-made – and one of them fitted me like a glove. I said 'I've never had something off-the-peg,' and he said 'We've been waiting for you!' That really rather summed it up ..."

The CD from Ace Records range of the old original Riverside Records has become a piece of folklore riveted into the 1955 season.

*Chapter 10*

# LANCIA'S
# SPA SWANSONG

Saddened teams gathered in the paddock before the Belgian Grand Prix at Spa, the first race since Ascari's death at Monza. Without their team leader, the exciting Lancia challenge seemed doomed or at least blunted. There were strong suggestions that the success of the Lancia D50s would somehow fuel the parlous financial situation the company found itself in and Ascari's fatal crash was seen as the signal of final commercial failure. It was thought that Lancia would not go to Spa in memory of Alberto, but young Eugenio Castellotti persuaded management that Ascari's memory would be better served by a Lancia presence at Spa. So two D50s were sent and Castellotti set out to learn a daunting circuit he had never seen before. It was only his fourth Grand Prix.

The modern Spa circuit is regarded with great respect by today's racing drivers but the original 8.75-mile road course was simply awesome, a course that certainly sorted the men from the boys in every racing generation. Just as the original Nürburgring mountain circuit just across the border had to be abandoned and replaced with a modern, safer sanitised circuit, so Spa was pruned and some of the more sensational corners like the kink at Masta, where an old farm building bent the road into a corner for road drivers but which was a flat-out challenge in a Formula 1 car, was consigned to exciting folklore.

Fangio held the lap record 4min 22.1sec (120.6mph/ 194.0kph) set four years before when he was driving for Alfa Romeo and it was Fangio who topped that record in the Mercedes on the first day of practice.

Mercedes had sent W196s for Fangio, Moss and Kling now recovered from his accident in the Mille Miglia. There were three Super Squalo Ferraris for Farina, lucky Monaco winner Trintignant and Paul Frère, the Belgian motoring journalist who was driving a works Ferrari for the first time. Four 250F Maseratis were entered for Behra, Musso, Mières and Perdisa. Mike Hawthorn was entered in a lone Vanwall and he was *not* happy in practice when team owner, G.A.Vandervell decided to drive the racing car to the circuit and wrecked the clutch in stop-start traffic.

Paul Frère's entry was tribute to an amazing performance by the motoring journalist who could race as well as he could write. He had raced Formula 1 cars for HWM and Gordini at Spa, his home track and in 1953 he had won a 24-hour touring car race round Spa in a Chrysler. Enzo Ferrari was always seeking fresh talent and he saw something special about the Belgian writer. Ferrari, had always fancied his own talents as a journalist, so he perhaps recognised a kindred spirit in the handsome, stylish Belgian driver. The offer was to drive at the Grands Prix of Monaco and Spa, but Frère felt that he would prefer to make his debut on a circuit he knew well, rather than face the special pressures at Monaco. Ferrari agreed, and entered Frère only as a reserve driver at Monaco, which meant that he practised but when Taruffi's Ferrari had lost many laps in the pits early in the race with a gearbox problem, Frère was sent out to drive to the finish gathering mileage and experience without any heroics being expected of him.

At Spa he felt at home and a year later in his memoirs *Un des Vingt au Depart*, translated into English as *On the Starting Grid* by the photographer Louis Klemantaski, he wrote of the moment before the start of the 1955 Grand Prix: "Knowing the circuit thoroughly and full of confidence in my brand-new car, I was fairly calm as I sat at the wheel waiting for the start of the race. And what a beautiful steering wheel it was too, made entirely of aluminium with a thin, overlaid, wooden rim and in its centre the famous escutcheon of the Rampant Horse!"

Frère would be the only journalist ever to race a Ferrari in a Grand Prix, indeed the only journalist ever to race in a Grand Prix, perhaps. In their later years Innes Ireland and Phil Hill would have their chance to display their ample abilities in *Autocar* and *Road & Track* respectively, after their retirements, but Paul Frère was the first to write first, race second.

The capricious weather in this area of the Ardennes simply added an aspect of unease and rain was dreaded. Spectators in the grandstands opposite the pits had a superb view of the majestic swoop down from the hairpin at La Source into the dip at Eau Rouge and the surge away up the hill beyond. Today the Michael Schumachers still regard the gravity-dipping dump into Eau Rouge where the bridge crosses an historic stream, as a challenge.

In the first session of practice on Thursday, Fangio slashed his lap record back to 4min 18.7sec and it would have been a brave man who suggested that anyone could beat that. Moss's best was 4min 24.4sec. Castellotti was finding his way with the Lancia round the superfast circuit, but on the second day he stunned the pit lane with a lap at 4min 18.1sec. It rained all day Saturday so Castellotti was guaranteed what would be the only pole position of his career. The front row saw a delighted Italian lining his Lancia up on the inside of the front row with Fangio and Moss in the W196s beside him. Farina's Ferrari and Behra's Maserati shared the second row.

Frère was as happy to qualify his Ferrari on the third row as Castellotti was to be on pole but Eugenio's race lasted barely half a lap as the Italian rookie discovered his D50 to be a different proposition on full tanks from how it had been with the minimum amount of fuel he had used for his pole lap. As the field streamed down from the slow corner at La Source between the grandstand and the pits, Fangio and Moss in the silver pair of Mercedes were well clear of the Lancia and the gap was opening. Moss had made a habit of shadowing Fangio as they ran 1–2 but at Spa Fangio was able to draw out something of a lead. Castellotti was dropping away in third place and being caught by Farina's Ferrari who had disposed of Kling's Mercedes on the way through. Behra had been fifth in the Maserati, battling with Kling and Frère, but he lost it and crashed backwards at high speed almost hitting the memorial stone to Richard Seaman who had been killed there in a Mercedes in the 1939 Grand Prix. Unperturbed, Behra ran to the pits and took over from Mières who was in pain from a sprained ankle.

After 16 laps of the 36-lap race, the colour went out of the event when Castellotti stopped with a wrecked crown wheel and pinion. Kling's Mercedes retired just after half distance with a broken oil pipe but Fangio and Moss were still well clear of the field and cruising to another 1–2 finish with Farina's Ferrari third, a minute and a half in arrears and extremely angry at the lack of competitiveness of his car. Frère, by comparison, was as ecstatic as his home crowd when he crossed the line in fourth place.

Paul Frère is still a respected motoring writer, now in his late 80s, and he would underline his smooth ability by finishing second at Le Mans in 1955 with a works Aston Martin, second again at Le Mans for Aston in 1959, winning the 24-hour race for Ferrari and the 12-hours of Reims, sharing with fellow-Belgian Olivier Gendebien in 1960.

Stirling Moss was relieved to take the chequered flag and keep his second place, 8sec adrift of his team leader because his W196 had suffered an oil leak in the closing laps and the floor of the cockpit was awash with lubricant. To add to his good fortune that Belgian afternoon, as the Mercedes mechanics pushed his car away after the race, a rear tyre went flat with a large nail embedded in the tread.

## Chapter 11

# LANCIA FLATTERS
# TO DEMISE

The D50 Lancia Grand Prix car was a technological shooting star in the motor racing firmament. It was the ultimate design from the drawing board of Vittorio Jano who had started in the racing department with Fiat in 1911, then moving to Alfa Romeo and designing the P2 GP car in the early 1920s. Jano also designed the legendary Tipo B or P3 Alfa which was driven by Tazio Nuvolari to a win at Monza first time out in 1933, and he would score another classic victory three years later in a P3 when he won on the Nürburgring in 1935, defeating the might of Mercedes and Auto Union in the Grand Prix on their own daunting mountain circuit. His victory was received in devastating silence.

The P2 was dominant in the 'twenties to the point in the 1924 Belgian Grand Prix at Spa when the Alfas were so far ahead that the crowd started to boo and jeer each time the P2s came down the hill past the pits, with Ascari and Campari miles in the lead of what must have turned into an extremely boring race. Jano signalled all his cars to stop at the pits together. He instructed the mechanics to take their time refuelling the cars and then clean and polish each one while the drivers sat down to a lunch that had been set up for them on tables in the pit lane. This was all *during* the race, you understand. The crowd responded with even more vigour.

Jano featured in the tortured superstition that hounded the Ascari family from father to son. Antonio Ascari won the 1924 Italian Grand Prix at Monza for Alfa Romeo at the wheel of Jano's new P2 and a year later he was killed in a P2 in the French Grand Prix. His young son Alberto was then just six years old. Thirty years later Alberto met his end in a racing car and his son Tonino was around the same age as his father had been when his grandfather was killed.

Jano's design of the D50 featured the first successful use of the V8 engine as a stressed member of the space frame chassis. It carried chassis loads from the top lugs at the back of the engine and the front suspension arms were attached to the front of the V8. That the V8 engine configuration itself was a first in Formula 1 is ironic as Coventry Climax had designed and built a V8 engine in 1953 for the new 2.5-litre formula in 1954 but had funked the challenge, spooked by rumours of overwhelming horsepower from European teams.

It would be 1967 before the Formula 1 world saw another V8 engine as a stressed member of the chassis when Colin Chapman built his monocoque Lotus Type 49 to take the new Cosworth DFV V8 designed by Keith Duckworth. In 1955 the V8 configuration was itself unique when other teams featured in-line eights, sixes or fours.

The Lancia pedigree in racing began early in the century when Vincenzo Lancia drove works FIAT cars and later built his own Lancia cars. His son Gianni was a free spirit, anxious to re-spark the family tradition in racing. He commissioned Jano to design a sports car which would grow into the D24 coupé driven by Umberto Maglioli to win the 1953 Targa Florio and Fangio would lead a 1–2–3 clean sweep for Lancia in the Carrera PanAmericana. In 1954 Ascari won the Mille Miglia and Taruffi won the Targa Florio in D24 sports cars now fitted with 3.3-litre engines.

Gianni's ambition was to move to the top rung of the racing ladder and Jano was working on the design of his trend-setting Grand Prix D50 with its distinctive pannier tanks slung between the front and rear wheels. The aim was to carry the fuel within the wheelbase and counter the change in handling as the fuel level reduced on a normal Grand Prix design of the day, with the fuel tank mounted in the tail behind the driver. There was also a measure of aerodynamic advantage by cleaning up the airflow between the wheels but this was in a time before wind tunnels, and the advantage could only be 'guesstimated'. Jano broke further new ground by incorporating the clutch with the five-speed gearbox rear-mounted in unit with the differential and forming part of the rear spaceframe. The V8 was mounted at an angle so that the drive-shaft ran down the left-hand side of the driver's seat and allowed him to sit lower in the car.

Lancia had contracted Alberto Ascari and his ageing friend, mentor and business partner, Luigi Villoresi, and both were happy to sign for the 1954 Grand Prix season but the debut of the new D50 was delayed for month succeeding month during the summer and Ascari and

Villoresi were released to drive for Maserati in the meantime.

The D50 appeared for the first time in the Spanish Grand Prix in October 1954 at Barcelona and Ascari flashed the promise of the advanced new design by taking pole, leading the early stages and then retiring with clutch problems.

The new car scored wins in non-title races early in 1955 when Ascari won the Naples GP and then the Turin GP, appropriately close to Lancia headquarters and wonderful for Gianni Lancia's ego. The fact that Mercedes had not attended either event was not considered important.

There had been suggestions that the new Lancias were amazingly fast in testing but also twitchy and only quick in the hands of those who knew them well.

Gianni thought big. He had commissioned a pair of huge transporters that doubled as well-equipped mobile workshops at the track, prototypes of the huge semi-trailers that are now arrayed in serried ranks in Grand Prix paddock areas. He also amazed other teams, including raising eyebrows at Mercedes-Benz who, it was felt, were re-writing the budget books in Formula 1. Lancia arranged for his D50 cars and team to be flown to Buenos Aires for the opening race of the season but Alberto spun into the wall and Luigi was out with fuel pump failure at half distance. It had been an expensive trip for zero results in the team's 1955 Grand Prix debut.

Better and worse was yet to come. Ascari was fast at Monaco during qualifying, setting a time that equalled Fangio's pole in the Mercedes. Castellotti was making his name with fourth fastest practice time and a place on the inside of the second row of the grid. He took the tussle to

Mercedes in the opening laps, but the Mercedes monopoly soon established itself at the front.

Gianni Lancia's Grand Prix aspirations literally sank with Ascari as the D50 smashed through the barriers on the outside of the quayside chicane and plunged into the harbour. Alberto had only just assumed the lead but he had yet to be signalled that Moss was out of the race and not still nearly a lap in front. It is part of racing history that Ascari survived relatively unscathed from the race that he would surely have won and achieved Gianni's greatest ambition. It could have possibly cemented ongoing arrangements for the team. While all looked rosy at the race track, things were not well back at the factory and while Gianni put on a brave face, in fact his company and especially his racing programme was about to unravel financially.

Ascari's untimely and freakish death while testing a Ferrari sports car a few days after his crash at Monaco, effectively spelt the end of Lancia in racing. The team withdrew but Castellotti persuaded management to send two cars to the Belgian Grand Prix at Spa where he lucked onto pole position (the final day was wet and did not allow a Mercedes challenge) but was a retirement in the race with transmission problems. It was all over.

History suggests that the team was offered to Mercedes who considered buying this item of opposition and closing it down to keep it out of reach of the very type of team that eventually came to own it. Maserati had apparently also been offered the Lancia operation but they felt that they were already in suitable shape and the acquirement of Lancia would be a complication they could cope without.

At the end of the 1955 season, after long procrastinations under the auspices of the Italian Automobile Club, the decision was taken to turn the whole Lancia racing organisation, engineers and equipment over to Enzo Ferrari. The arrangement reminded historians of Alfa Romeo withdrawing and handing its racing team to Ferrari in the early 1930s.

The arrangement solved several problems. Ferrari was in dire trouble endeavouring to survive one of his team's more spectacularly historic cyclical downturns. The deed included 50-million Lira a year for five years which worked out at a total budget of £128,000 which is nominal now but was *manna* from heaven for Ferrari then.

The official statement read:

*With the intention of promoting the technical advancement of racing cars, which are part of the glorious tradition of the Italian motor industry and add prestige to Italian products throughout the world, the President General of the Italian Automobile Club has decided to intervene personally with Fiat and Lancia to enlist their help in supporting Automobili Ferrari.*

We have seen that Ferrari had been clutching at technical straws to the point where he had commissioned the design and making of a *twin cylinder* 2.5-litre as a desperation measure to succeed at Monaco. As it turned out, fate decreed that he would win the jewel in the Grand Prix crown that summer by sheer fluke when Trintignant won with a clearly outdated Ferrari after all the favoured runners had failed. The gift of the Lancia team was the answer to his prayers.

The cars appeared for the first time as part of the Scuderia Ferrari at Monza late in 1955 but they had been designed by Jano specifically for Pirelli tyres and on Ferrari's contracted Engleberts the cars were a total handful and dangerous. With the threat of blow-outs on the bankings they were withdrawn to return and win the following summer.

Ironically, most of Jano's technical design novelties were stripped by him, piece by piece, from the cars once they had been moved to Modena and re-named Lancia-Ferraris. Power went up by 20bhp to 290bhp. Coil springs replaced leaves in the front suspension. The engine no longer formed a stressed part of the chassis. The panniers were stripped of their main purpose with the main fuel tank now in the tail as tradition seemed to insist, and the distinctive shapely side tanks were now only reserve capacity if required. They would soon disappear altogether and an era had then officially been erased.

The success that had eluded Gianni Lancia, perversely came in the summer of 1956 when Fangio would drive the revamped and renamed D50s to wins in Argentina, Britain and Germany, seconds in Monaco and Monza (after the personal gift of Peter Collins' car) and taking the World Championship.

Gianni would have done his best to be delighted.

Vittorio Jano stayed with Ferrari and would design and/or develop the Dino V6 engine. Ferrari folklore would like to believe that Enzo's son Dino had either designed the engine or certainly worked on it and when he died Enzo went into a decline. He visited his son's grave every day and his office was gloomily lit only over the photo of

Dino. Jano, who had been close to Ferrari since the Alfa Romeo days in the 'twenties, lost his own son in 1966, and in his sorrow he committed suicide, aged 75.

*Chapter 12*

# NEW BRITISH CARS
# AT LE MANS

Two new cars, or to be correct, two sports cars were developed from racing prototypes to be launched in events during the summer of 1955. The shape of the MGA had been seen at Le Mans in 1951 as a factory prototype raced by George Phillips, whose day job was motor racing photographer for *Autosport*. The Austin-Healey 100S was a limited production model based on a prototype raced at Sebring in 1954. Both cars originated from beneath the British Motor Corporation umbrella.

The MG was a racing special that became a hugely popular road car while the 100S was a racing special based on the road-going Austin-Healey 100/4.

There would be more MGAs sold than the total production of all the MG models before it and yet it was greeted by a mixture of awe and disbelief. MG traditionalists were prepared to hate it. The new 'A' was obviously the end of the traditional square-rigged MG radiator that was so much a part of the marque's history. The shapely new body was a 1950s automotive equivalent of the 'New Look' in fashion circles. I can remember as a schoolboy in 1955, thinking that MG had lost its way with the 'A'. It was almost feminine, a hairdresser's car rather than any sort of racing machine. The TC-TD-TF line had ground to a halt. The octagon marque image was being dragged into the second half of the century.

In fact the spark of the shape of the new MG had been hatched by Reid Railton in the late 1930s when he clothed 'Goldie' Gardner's supercharged K3 – an ultimate piece of upright MG history – in a slippery aerodynamic shape for record breaking. The MGA borrowed from those sleek lines.

Phillips had converted a TC to race at Le Mans in 1949 and 1950 with sufficient success to prompt MG's Syd Enever to design a new streamlined body along the family lines of Gardner's record-breaker. Sharing the drive with Eric Winterbottom in 1950 Phillips finished a creditable second in the 1.5-litre class, averaging 73mph (117.5kph) so he knew what was required when he ran the stream-lined TD-based car at Le Mans in 1951. On the Mulsanne Straight, the new car with its unsupercharged 1,250cc four-cylinder XPAG engine would top 115mph (185kph) but three hours into the 24-hour race the top came off a piston and the engine was wrecked. Phillips was renowned as a man who never suffered fools at all, never mind gladly, and he was furious, blaming MG for poor engine preparation. The company felt that Phillips and co-driver Alan Rippon, had been running too hard so early in the long race. Phillips was apparently offered the streamlined prototype but he refused the gesture and the car was broken up.

Putting the prototype under the wrecker's hammer sounds a trifle extreme today, but it had served its purpose and another development model was complete by the end of 1952, a car that mirrored the first prototype and would stand as the image for the first MGA production car when it was finally launched at Earls Court in October 1955.

Four MGAs were entered for Le Mans in June 1955, prepared by the new competition department headed by Alec Hounslow who had ridden with the great Tazio Nuvolari when he won the Tourist Trophy race on the Ards circuit near Belfast in 1932. Hounslow was from the old school of race preparation and insisted that every nut and bolt on the cars was lock-wired. The four cars looked identical to the cars that would be offered for sale later in the year, but the bodies were in aluminium, fixed with countersunk rivets. The engines were four-cylinder 1.5-litre B-series modified to give 82.5bhp at 6,000rpm compared with 68bhp from the standard MGA at its official announcement later in the year.

Three prototypes were entered with a fourth car taken across as a spare. The driver pairings were Ken Miles/Johnny Lockett, Dick Jacobs/Joe Flynn and Ted Lund/Hans Waeffler. Soon after the Levegh crash, at 6.39pm, Dick Jacobs came out of White House on the wrong camber, slid and went into a ditch overturning and catching fire. Jacobs was badly injured and never raced again. The car was burned out. It was suggested that he had been distracted by the enormity of the accident a little further up the track.

The Lockett/Miles car finished 12th overall and 5th in class at an average of 86.17mph (138.6kph); the Lund/Waeffler car had tagged a D-type and lost time in the pits for repairs, finishing 17th and sixth in class, having set fastest MG timed speed on the Mulsanne

Straight at 119.5mph (192.3kph). Plans had been made to enter these cars in the Alpine Rally but the event was cancelled as a legacy of the Le Mans crash.

The next outing for these works MGs was in the TT at Dundrod in September but the team seemed to fall foul of in-house company politics. Two twin-cam versions of the B-series engine had been produced, one from Morris was fitted in the 12th place Le Mans car, the other from Austin was in the 17th placed 'A'. At the last minute, and in a move that has wrong-footed race historians since then, the Austin twin-cam engine with its 66° layout, was removed and replaced by a B-series pushrod engine. That one-off twin-cam was crated and never seen again.

The Morris twin-cam, driven by Ron Flockhart and Johnny Lockett, went well in the TT until a misfire set in and the car was out after 23 laps. The Ted Lund/Dickie Stoop car was out after only eight laps with a split experimental fuel tank. The survivor, now stripped of its twin-cam engine, placed fourth in class behind three Porsches.

The Healey 100S was the ultimate competition version of the sports car Donald Healey had wanted when he did the deal with Leonard Lord and Austin to build the Austin-Healey 100/4. It was an out-and-out road racer with an up-rated engine featuring an aluminium 'Weslake' head, a competition gearbox, improved dampers, Dunlop disc brakes instead of standard drums, a light-alloy body replacing standard steel, a full-width racing screen, bonnet louvres, bonnet anchoring strap and clips, no hood or side screens, no bumpers and a svelte oval grille with the 'S' badge. A large racing-type filler cap fed the 20-gallon (91-litre) petrol tank that dominated the boot. A stylish two-tone colour scheme featured white on dark blue, for many the American racing colours. A plaque on the dash of all 52 100S models built, read: "This car is a replica of the Austin-Healey '100' (Sebring) which averaged 132.29mph (212.9kph) for 24 hours and was officially timed by the American Automobile Association at a mean speed of 143.1mph (230.2kph) over the measured mile at Bonneville, Utah. U.S.A. August 1954." Added was Donald Healey's signature with the address: Warwick, England.

I suppose 100S (for Sebring) reads better in retrospect than 100B (for Bonneville). In fact Donald Healey had wanted to call this competition model the Austin-Healey Sebring but was prevented from so doing by the fact that Frazer Nash had already registered the model name.

The first prototype of the 100S – known at Healey as Special Test Vehicles – ran in the Sebring 12-hour race in 1954 where they finished third overall and first in class and gathered enough kudos to trigger the 1955 production run at Warwick. Lance Macklin and George Huntoon finished third to the OSCA of Moss/Lloyd and the Lancia of Rubirosa. Moss was completely without clutch or brakes in the last four hours. In fact the Healey was in a strong second place when a rocker arm broke and after a pit-stop to remove the broken pieces, the car ran to the finish on three cylinders. Harry Weslake had broken a rocker arm on the test bed a few days before the Sebring race ...

Lance Macklin was a pivotal personality in the Healey 100S saga. He was a British driver who missed the main chance, a charismatic young man who was leading the HWM team in the early 1950s when Stirling Moss arrived. They were similar personalities, both young, handsome, sporty bachelors, eager to race and with a practised eye for a pretty girl. Moss would say that he learned to race from HWM and learned about life from Lance Macklin. In *Stirling Moss* published in 1953, Robert Raymond wrote of those HWM days: "Both Moss and Macklin were prone to assume that they were finished, all washed up, if within three hours of arriving in a new town, they had not both been out to dinner with the two prettiest girls in the neighbourhood."

Lance was the son of Sir Noel Macklin who had founded and funded the Invicta and Railton road car projects. Lance's first racing car after the war was an Invicta. He raced for HWM in Formula 1 and Formula 2 for three seasons with a best finish of 8th in the Dutch GP, six laps behind the leader, Ascari in the works Ferrari. In 1953 he raced the HWM in six GPs and failed to finish in any of them!

Moss had a high regard for Macklin's ability, perhaps seeing something of himself in his friend, and he made his own 250F Maserati available to him. In 1955 Lance raced in two GPs in the 250F with Stirling Moss Ltd as entrant. He failed to qualify at Monaco and finished 8th in the British GP at Aintree, 11 laps behind his winning entrant.

Moss and Macklin drove together in a 100S at Sebring in 1955 with the car now officially entered as a 100S with the 'S' scroll badge on the special oval grille. Stirling had a passing comment on this race, noting that Macklin had driven the car down from New York and arrived with "an interesting collection of speeding tickets." There were seven 100S models entered and the Moss/Macklin car was easily fastest, finishing sixth overall and class winner, behind a D-type Jaguar, two Ferraris and two Maseratis.

Three works 100Ss were entered for the 1955 Mille Miglia with Moss otherwise and more successfully engaged up front with Mercedes-Benz. A fourth 100S was entered for Ron Flockhart. Donald Healey and Jim Cashmore shared a 100S fitted with weather equipment but made so many stops for oil that they finished outside the time limit. It would be Donald's last race, his entry allowed only under sufferance by the company's account-ants. George Abecassis had a red 100S which ran out of fuel in the mountains before Rome. A spectator helped with a reserve supply but he had lost valuable time (52 places on the Aquila–Rome section) and would survive to win his class and finish 11th overall. Macklin had been fastest 100S driver in the opening stages but suffered a broken throttle control and drove the final stages on the ignition switch, finishing 36th overall. Flockhart crashed through a bridge parapet into the riverbed below, scram-bled out of the wreck and was carried to a nearby home where he was stripped and rubbed down with Italian brandy. When Geoffrey Healey arrived some hours later to collect him he was completely recovered ... inside and out.

Carroll Shelby told a similar tale from his 100S entry in the 1954 Carrera PanAmericana where he was to share a car with Roy Jackson-Moore, Healey's representative in North America and sometime racing driver who remem-bered their car as "a 100/4 with 'S' bits, different wheels and tyres. We were aiming at 140mph on the long straights in Mexico. Carroll and I had a few differences of opinion but of course he was a better driver than I was."

Shelby remembers that Carrera with hoots of laughter. "I was to drive one leg and Roy would drive the other. On the first day they wanted me to ride with him but I said I wouldn't drive with *anyone* on a thing like the Carrera. They finally talked me into it and he drove half the first leg. I was with him in the car and he was *petrified* of those little narrow roads in the mountains. That night I told Donald Healey I wasn't going to ride with Jackson-Moore, and Roy said 'Well, I'm not going to ride with you either, 'cause you're *crazy!*' I decided I'd make sure he didn't come with me and I took the passenger's seat out ...

"So I started out and I was going to make up some time. I was goin' like hell, passing all the Lincolns and Chryslers ... then I hit the 150 kilometre marker. That marker post stuffed right through the tonneau cover where old Jackson-Moore would have bin. I lost it in a big way. Went end over end. The knock-off wheel hammer came loose. It was bolted on and I hit the goddam rock so hard that it broke the hammer handle off at the head and y'know *that* takes some leverage! The head of the hammer smashed my elbow to hell. There were two schoolteachers from Brooklyn working their way down to Guatemala on holiday and they had a bottle of brandy with 'em, so they came down and then an Indian came down with a bucket of Mexican beer. So I just sat there on this blanket and by the time the ambulance came several hours later, I didn't care about *anythin'*. I was as smashed as my elbow ..."

Chapter 13

# DISASTER AT LE MANS

REUTERS, LE MANS JUNE 12:

*Le Mans lowered its shutters and drew its blinds in mourning today for the eighty-four people killed when the blazing wreckage of a Mercedes sports car sliced through the crowd two hours after the start of the twenty-four hour endurance race.*

*About seventy-seven people were injured. Some are so desperately ill it is feared the death toll will rise still further. Today weeping relatives filed through the hospitals, clinics and morgue at the little French provincial town in a grisly identification parade of the unnamed victims.*

*Some of the men, women and children killed were so terribly mutilated that they may never be recognised.*

*Messages of sympathy poured in, led by two from the West German President (Professor Theodor Heuss) and the Chancellor (Dr Konrad Adenauer). The French Prime Minister (Mr Edgar Faure) is in close touch with the local authorities.*

*The record crowd packed around the rails were in gay carnival mood when the crash occurred – the worst in motor racing history.*

*Eye-witnesses said that Mike Hawthorn, of Britain, who went on to win the race, was signalled into the Jaguar pits to refuel.*

*Lance Macklin, in an Austin-Healey, swerved hard with
screaming tyres to avoid the (other) British car.*

## No Escape

*The veteran French driver, Pierre Levegh, chasing the leaders at
125 miles an hour, could not avoid Macklin's car.*

*His silver Mercedes glanced off the side of it and, with an
earth-shaking roar, exploded like a fire-bomb, showering white-
hot sparks into the air.*

*Its engine and other parts slashed like a scythe through the
packed crowd. In the split second it took to happen, few people in
the packed enclosure had time to duck. Most were cut down
where they stood.*

*Hundreds of spectators dashed up to help the rescue teams,
police and firemen. A black-robed priest moved slowly among the
dying, administering the Last Sacraments.*

*Levegh, killed instantly, was dragged from the blazing tangle
that had been his car.*

*Other bodies were carried away on stretchers and ladders.
Most of the killed were French.*

## 'Worse Than War'

*Most of the injuries in hospital had skull injuries, a doctor said.
One of the injured, Mr Jacques Lelong, said: "It was worse than
the war. I saw a little girl trampled on in the panic and stricken
spectators lying in pools of blood.*

*I saw a headless man beside me collapse like a rag doll."*

*On the other side of the track it was several hours before many
people knew of the crash as they danced in the open air and rode
the fun fair roundabouts.*

*They first heard of it when the Mercedes team withdrew at
two o'clock in the morning as a mark of respect for the victims.*

### Saved Life

*The winner, Mike Hawthorn, said after the race that it was the 'toughest grind' of his career.*

*The World Champion, Juan Fangio, of Argentina, said that Levegh saved his (Fangio's) life just before crashing.*

*"I was doing 260 kilometres an hour (162 miles an hour) when Levegh suddenly raised his hand. He was warning me of some danger I could not see.*

*"I braked, but at that speed there was no question of pulling up in a few metres. How I got through and missed Macklin, I don't know."*

*Fangio was so close to the blazing car that his windscreen cracked.*

The Le Mans disaster completely dominated the remainder of the 1955 season so there is no apology for reprinting the Reuters coverage that beamed the news around the world.

Blame was spread widely. That Hawthorn's Jaguar had passed Macklin's Healey and then cut across, causing him to swerve. That Macklin triggered the crash by swerving into the path of Levegh's approaching Mercedes. That Levegh was too old, at 49, to be driving such a fast car. Jaguar team manager Lofty England strenuously defended the suggestion that Hawthorn had made a last-minute decision to make a pit-stop; he had been signalled to come in on count-down over the previous few laps.

*Was* Levegh too old to be in the Mercedes? *Why* was he in the Mercedes team? It seems that it was something of a PR exercise to use a French driver in the German team's line up and many felt it was a belated thank you for Levegh presenting Mercedes with the 24-hour race on a plate in 1952 when his Talbot broke its crankshaft with only an hour to go. Levegh had been the French hero for 23 hours in that race as he drove single-handed and held a comfortable lead over the two Mercedes 300SLs running in second and third places. It has to be appreciated that in those days, as now to a lesser degree, Le Mans was *the* French national summer passion, up there with the Tour de France. When the Talbot failed, the famous 24-hour race became a Mercedes 1–2 victory. When the Talbot failed, Levegh went instantly from hero to zero in the eyes of the fickle French crowd.

Levegh was a complicated personality, a driver who felt pressured by family history to succeed in motor racing. His uncle, Pierre Levegh, had been a racing 'name' in France at the turn of the century but there had been no other male to carry on the family tradition, until the famous driver's sister, a Madame Bouillin, had a son and named him Pierre. He was born in 1905 soon after his uncle's retirement and grew up with the family legend. Eventually the family made the decision that the boy would adopt the name of his uncle and Pierre Bouillin legally became Pierre Levegh in the hope that family fortune would somehow repeat.

In fact this was the third name change in the family saga. The racing uncle's real name, according to period racer Charles Jarrott, was Velghe but he raced as 'Levegh'!

In his splendid book *Ten Years of Motors and Motor Racing 1896–1906* Jarrott wrote: "The name of Levegh and Mors were indicative of a formidable combination in any race and the splendid performances achieved by him, particularly in the Paris-Toulouse-Paris race, stamped him as a Speed King. The first time I met him was in a paper-chase in which I took part in France in 1898. Driving a Mors car, he was endeavouring to make up speed at the finish in the Forest of St. Germain. He had a lady passenger with him, and as he whizzed by we were amazed to see Levegh and his passenger sitting on the floor in order to save 'windage' [sic] , and thus increase their speed to some fractional extent, and Levegh was steering the car, holding on to the steering-bar above his head. What he did when he wished to stop, I do not know – presumably he resumed his proper seat first."

Young Pierre grew up with the history of Le Mans having been in the crowd at the first race in 1923. It was his burning ambition to win. He excelled as a mechanic and eventually gained a drive in the fifth of six Talbots entered by Tony Lago in 1938. The car failed before he had the chance to take the wheel. In 1951 he was back again, and again in the fifth of six Talbots, sharing with René Marchand. They finished this time, in fourth place. Levegh was in his mid-forties but he believed that age and experience were more important than youth and enthusiasm in a race that blasted twice round the clock. His time would come.

Levegh invested his life savings in a new 4½-litre 1951 Talbot and prepared it meticulously for the 1952 Le Mans race. Rather than be fifth in a six-car team, he would be number one in his own team. René Marchand was his co-driver once again.

The mechanical trauma began seven hours into the race, when Levegh, proudly leading his precious race, noted an abnormal engine vibration and decided that one of the crankshaft bearings had gone. He was right. One of the bolts on the central crankshaft bearing had fractured and fallen into the sump without causing any damage. Levegh told W.F. Bradley, veteran European-based *Autocar* journalist the inside details of that awful 1952 race but he never wrote about it until after Levegh's death at Le Mans three years later.

"'If I stop,' Levegh told himself in 1952, 'and turn the car over to my team-mate it will be known that my engine is crippled; the Mercedes team will speed up and the race will be lost. There is only one hope. I must drive to the end and keep my mouth shut.' The time came to change drivers, but Levegh pushed his team-mate aside with the remark. 'I am going on.'

"'Fool,' was the general comment. 'He thinks he can drive twenty-four hours without help. He is just throwing the race away to the Germans.'

"On Sunday morning the Talbot's rev counter failed and Levegh was aware that the engine vibration had increased and in all probability the crankshaft had begun to fracture.

"By two o'clock on Sunday afternoon Levegh had such a lead that it appeared impossible for the Germans to catch him. He slowed down a little; he listened to the beat of his engine almost in agony. Would it go to the end? He doubted it, but hoped for the best. Most important of all, nobody outside should have an inkling of his trouble – his distress.

"Three o'clock on Sunday afternoon. Only one hour to go. The Talbot had outrun all its rivals and had such a lead that it could afford to cruise around and still come in ahead. In the Press stand we had started our final reports, centred around the exploit of Pierre Levegh, leaving blanks for the total distance and the average speed.

THE AMAZING SUMMER OF '55

"Fifty minutes to go and the Talbot pulled into the pits; Levegh staggered out, fell into the arms of his wife and burst into tears. The crankshaft had broken, the car was a wreck and the man who had tenderly nursed it nearly twice round the clock had broken down with emotion.

"This Levegh, this silent, tight-lipped Frenchman sought to do something that no man had ever accomplished. He imagined that he, of all men, could drive at racing speeds for twenty-four consecutive hours. He had no rev counter; he was unnecessarily racing his engine; he was worn out, exhausted by super-human effort dictated by his inherent pride. He had made a gift of the first prize to the German team.

"Not a word passed his lips. The flood of criticism swept over him, leaving him apparently indifferent. The rules were changed to make it impossible for any man to attempt to drive throughout the twenty-four hours. Anthony Lago carried the broken bearing bolt, with the fracture clearly visible, in his pocket for a couple of years and presented it as the explanation of the failure of his car to win the race. But of the heroism of the driver, his stubborn determination, the agony he endured hour after hour, not a syllable was revealed. It is only now that he has gone – his final gesture before he passed into eternity being to raise his arm to warn his team-mate Fangio of the danger which lay immediately ahead – that the story of the silent hero can be told ..."

Jaguar history was missed when Jimmy Stewart, elder brother of young Jackie, went off the road while doing pre-Le Mans testing of a D-type at the Nürburgring. The car rolled down a bank and it was 25 minutes before he was rescued, pinned under the car and drenched in petrol. He suffered only slight injury but it was to the arm which was badly damaged at Le Mans the year before. Jimmy made the decision to quit racing. His place in the works D-type for the 24-hour race was taken by Ivor Bueb, sharing with Mike Hawthorn ...

In 1955, the Le Mans course on public roads was 13 kilometres 492 metres – 8.385 statute miles – long before the chicanes that would reduce the ultimate velocity of the fastest cars down the l-o-n-g Mulsanne Straight ... and before the safety modifications that would be introduced in the bruising aftermath of this race.

A few years ago I was lucky enough to passenger veteran Belgian writer/racer Paul Frère for several laps of the track on race morning in the same yellow Equipe National Belge D-type Jaguar that Belgian drivers Johnny Claes and Jacques Swaters drove to fourth place in 1955. After the pits the track swept right under the Dunlop Bridge, up and over the crest of the hill and down into the Esses. Wind up again to Tertre Rouge and then the blast down past the Café de l'Hippodrome to Mulsanne corner. Mulsanne was a slow right hander where drivers had the time to scan the signalling pits out there in the country on the far side of the track from the pits. The road was then a series of linked straights to Indianapolis, curving into Arnage. After Arnage there are still gentle curves and straights linked by slight curves. The famous White House corner reminded historians of the 1927 race when the Bentley team was almost written off in one major accident.

Count Maggi of the Brescia Automobile Club and founder of the Mille Miglia was the honorary starter of the Le Mans race in 1955. Among the national flags, the

Italian colours were flying at half mast in memory of Alberto Ascari.

The 1955 race started at storming speed with the 4.4-litre Ferraris of Castellotti and Maglioli out in front. Fangio's Mercedes and Hawthorn's D-type had made tardy starts. Hawthorn was pampering a newly-fitted motor; Fangio had inadvertently slipped the gearlever up his trouser-leg ... The pair soon came through to the front, smashing lap records and swapping the lead, lap after lap.

The Mercedes pace was aided by the full-width air-drag brake in the tail, a 20-inch high windowed panel running the width of the car behind the cockpit. It was operated hydraulically from the cockpit, rising from the tail and dragging off speed to aid braking. The hydraulic rams were worked by a lever placed above the gear change. The drivers discovered that a touch of flap also aided downforce adhesion out of corners. Moss inadvertently left the flap up as he tried to accelerate away from Mulsanne and found the car so dead that he thought he had blown the engine.

After two hours the race *average* of 118.9mph (191.3kph) was faster than the 1954 lap record. Twenty-six minutes later came the carnage when Levegh's Mercedes launched off the tail of Macklin's Austin-Healey and into the crowd below the grandstand and across the road from the pits.

Eric Thompson was standing on the pit counter waiting to take over the 1½-litre Connaught from Ken McAlpine and was sighting down the track to spot him coming in. "I didn't register Hawthorn going by but I saw Lance Macklin in the Austin-Healey moments before Levegh hit

him and the Mercedes somersaulted over the earth barri-
cade. Chaos ensued with mechanics and marshals
running across the road and with the racing cars threading their way through the debris. From pit level we could-
n't see the carnage in the spectator area. The Connaught
came in, refuelled and I took over. It was only when I was
approaching the pits after White House that the enormity
of the accident became evident with a vast plume of
smoke rising into the air. For once, motor racing didn't
seem like fun ..."

Hawthorn was distraught and all for retiring there and
then but Lofty England calmed him, assuring the
Englishman that he was in no way to blame, and the
Jaguar team manager would strenuously defend
Hawthorn's part in the accident to the end of his days. He
said that a new engine had been fitted in Hawthorn's car
before the race and he had been asked to take it easy in
the opening laps. Castellotti's Ferrari enjoyed an early
lead but he was hauled in by the Jaguar and Mercedes
and in the ensuing battle Hawthorn set a new lap record
giving him a clear lead over Fangio on the lap before his
scheduled pit-stop to re-fuel.

"On the lap on which the accident took place Hawthorn
was due to make a routine re-fuelling stop, of which he
had been given warning by signals from our pit for three
laps before the actual stop – this being our standard
practice," England wrote. "There was, therefore, no
question of his making a sudden or unexpected stop. At
this time Hawthorn was leading the race and I would say
was then some 10 seconds ahead of Fangio. Between
Arnage and White House corner he had passed Macklin
(Austin-Healey) and, when clear of Macklin, drew across

to the right side of the road and started braking to pull up at the pit in the normal fashion.

"While this was going on, Kling (Mercedes) had pulled out before White House corner to go into the pit with some throttle linkage trouble, leaving Levegh on his own for the first time since the early part of the race – having followed Kling round consistently for several laps.

"At the same time Fangio (Mercedes) was immediately behind Levegh coming out of White House corner and about to pass him. It is my belief that Levegh, anticipating Fangio to pass before the pit area, pulled across to the middle of the road to leave room for Fangio and was obviously keeping a close watch on his mirror to see what Fangio was doing. Macklin had no doubt observed Levegh coming up very fast behind him, and was therefore keeping a watch in his mirror to see what Levegh intended to do prior to pulling out to pass Hawthorn.

"Thus, the attention of these two drivers may have been diverted from what was going on ahead of them by what was happening in the rear – resulting in Macklin finding himself closing up rapidly on Hawthorn and then braking heavily and turning out to pass Hawthorn. At the same time, Levegh found himself in a position where he was too late to take avoiding action to miss Macklin and ran over the back of his car.

"This assessment of the possible sequence of events leading up to the accident was made for me from Mike Hawthorn's own report and from my knowledge of the position of the various cars in the race at that time and from reports we received from a number of spectators who wrote to us following the accident; none of whom, incidentally, made any suggestion that the fault was Hawthorn's!"

Macklin's car was launched into a wild clockwise spin into the left bank, bouncing back across the track to hit the pit wall and lurching back to the left-hand side of the track again. Fangio, meanwhile, had amazingly threaded his way through the erratic gap being wrought by Macklin. The distraught Hawthorn had overshot his pit and climbed out of the Jaguar in case other cars struck the wreckage in the track. England told Hawthorn to complete another lap because they could not change drivers if they were not at their own pit.

From other accounts, Hawthorn, in the eye of the storm and being accused of causing the crash in its immediate aftermath, was all for quitting the race ... even his career ... at that point, but the Jaguar team manager was able to calm him and convince him that he was not to blame for the largest and worst accident in motor racing history.

Paul Frère is of the opinion that it was fate that the accident would never have happened if he, Frère, had been in a position to take up the offer of a Le Mans drive made by Neubauer in December 1954. By then he had already agreed a drive with Aston Martin, so Neubauer then contacted Levegh. In his 1956 autobiography *On the Starting Grid*, Frère writes of the accident: "To establish a scale of responsibilities, one would have to know in what measure the second car (Macklin's) had been baulked by the first car (Hawthorn's) stopping at its pit; whether, in fact, Macklin could not have avoided making the sudden swerve which Hawthorn's action had provoked; and if, in some measure, the driver of the Mercedes had not, himself, been caught napping by the incident which perhaps he should have anticipated. Most probably

Macklin had his attention distracted by the approach of Fangio's and Levegh's Mercedes from behind. Not wishing to impede them, he was looking in his rear-view mirror, which would explain how he could have been surprised by Hawthorn's action..." Frère explains Neubauer's offer of the drive that then went to Levegh and observes "One thing is certain – that had it been me at the wheel of the car, it would not have been at the same spot at that fatal moment..."

Stirling Moss had taken over from Fangio in the leading Mercedes and Peter Garnier captured the scene of the on-going race in *Autocar*: "The sunlight went from the sky, the Esso balloon man hung limp as the evening chill cooled his innards. High cirrus promised a fine night. That sad figure of the death toll from the crash had not yet been disclosed... Stop lights began to glow in the evening and the noise of the Offenhauser engine in the Cunningham and Johnson car challenged the penetrating howl of the 1½-litre McAlpine and Thompson Connaught. There would be no peace this June evening."

By midnight the Fangio/Moss Mercedes was two laps clear of the Hawthorn/Bueb D-type with Kling/Simon Mercedes in third. Two hours later and the tragic death toll from the accident had been announced to a hushed crowd in the darkness, many of whom on the other side of the circuit were unaware that it had happened. Then came the announcement relayed from the board room at Mercedes in Stuttgart, that a decision had been taken to withdraw the team from the race as a mark of respect. Thus the cars running first and third were removed from the running. There were those who questioned the organisers in allowing the race to continue after the disastrous crash, but this was defended on grounds that the rescue services would have been overwhelmed if the surrounding roads were suddenly swamped with spectators. It was also suggested that Jaguar should also have withdrawn but it was reckoned that this would have been to assume some sort of responsibility for the crash, which team manager Lofty England strenuously denied.

Stirling Moss was angry that their leading car had been pulled out. "There was no way the SLR was going to break," he wrote in *My Cars, My Career*. "I think it was poor Levegh's co-driver John Fitch who suggested to Mercedes management they should withdraw in respect for those who had died. But that struck me as a rather empty theatrical gesture which came close to accepting some responsibility for what had happened. It achieved nothing except hand a very prestigious race on a plate to Jaguar. Time has not altered my view, and I was very frustrated when we were ordered to withdraw at 2am Sunday morning."

All the Ferraris had retired. At half distance, four o'clock on Sunday morning, the order ran: Jaguar–Maserati–Aston Martin–Jaguar-Porsche–Porsche. At 7am Collins in the Aston Martin overtook the Maserati for second place, four laps behind the leading Jaguar, but Musso/Valenzano fought back and the Italian car re-took second place. It would be claimed by clutch failure a few hours later.

And so Mike Hawthorn and Ivor Bueb, the last minute replacement for Jackie Stewart's brother Jimmy, won the troubled 24-hour race for Jaguar, a victory that seemed to many to be totally academic. Surely Mercedes would have won if the team had not been withdrawn after the decision of the directors. The Mercedes people found themselves in the invidious position of being damned if they did and damned if they didn't. On balance, they chose to withdraw which gifted the race to Jaguar.

*(Translation of report by Alfred Neubauer. Translator's note: the German – 1950s – style is slightly ponderous, and no attempt was made to translate this into 'modern' English)*

### Alfred Neubauer, Race Manager

The tragedy at the Le Mans 24-hour race in 1955 as seen by the Race Manager of Daimler-Benz AG

### 1. Observations

As the race proceeded, drivers Fangio on Mercedes-Benz and Hawthorn on Jaguar were out in the lead. These two drivers raced at such a high speed that as early as the 36th lap, about two-and-a-half hours into the race, they were expected to lap the other two Mercedes-Benz drivers Kling (start no. 21) and Levegh (start no. 20).

It was therefore with extra concentration that I myself and my time-keeping assistant, Mr. Geier, waited for the cars to pass by the next time and saw the accident happen. When the expected pack of leading cars turned into the straight past the grandstand, having passed through a flat bend, the first to appear were two green cars, followed closely by an aluminum-colored car; however, the start numbers of all these cars were not clearly discernible from a distance of about 150 meters (164 yards). Suddenly and completely unexpectedly, the aluminium-colored car, moving closely along the protective edging of the racetrack, lifted off the ground, some three to four meters (10–13 feet) high, and was thrown across the protective embankment into the area where spectators were standing next to the grandstand. The car did not catch fire before it had come to a standstill.

In the pits, we immediately thought that this could only have been Kling or Levegh because Fangio had passed the pits only fractions of a second earlier and had been properly registered in our lists with a driving time of four minutes and 17 seconds. Hardly had Fangio shot past the pits when the lighter of the two green cars with start no. 26 (Macklin on Austin-Healey) skidded transversely across the racetrack from the far left to the right-hand side of the track, straight towards our first pit, where it seriously injured two people, bounced off, skidded across the track again and crashed into the inner wall, where it came to a stop. The driver jumped out of the car and ran away. Mechanics subsequently tried to move this car back to the right-hand edge of the track outside the pits by means of roller jacks. The car's bodywork was torn apart at the rear left-hand side, and the rear wire-spoke wheel on the left was without tube and tire; the latter were, however, found outside the Mercedes-Benz pit.

## 2. Comments by driver Kling

In the evening after the race, Herr Kling reported the following: He had a problem with the accelerator pedal on his car and therefore drove slowly to come into the pits. While going more slowly, he let drivers Levegh and Fangio pass. He subsequently dropped behind so far that he saw neither the accident nor its causes nor, with the exception of the fire, its consequences. Since burning fuel was flowing across the track, Herr Kling stopped the car completely and, when there was no longer any danger, drove slowly to the pits to have the defective throttle valve repaired. It should therefore be expressly noted that Herr Kling did not see how the disaster happened.

### 3. Comments by driver Fangio

Herr Fangio confirmed the situation immediately before the tragedy as follows: Hawthorn was out in the lead, driving along the inner edge of the track, and had overtaken Levegh. Fangio himself was just behind Levegh when the latter suddenly and unexpectedly raised his right arm, apparently to warn the drivers behind him. Fangio understood instantly that at this point of the racetrack, just before the straight past the grandstand, a severe accident was imminent. He therefore steered his car to the right, thereby negotiating the entire group, which was to become involved in the accident, on the inner side of the racetrack (seen in clockwise direction). Fangio was unable to see how many – and which – cars were about to crash since the disaster happened when he was already some 100 meters (110 yards) away from that point. Hence, Fangio did not watch the accident itself. He is, however, convinced that Levegh saved his life by warning him.

### 4. Logical conclusion

Macklin's car with start no. 26 caused the accident of Levegh's car by reducing its speed so abruptly that

148

Levegh's car crashed into the rear of Macklin's car. As already mentioned, Levegh's car lifted off, flying through the air at an angle and turning slightly to the left, across the sand embankment and against the wall behind which the spectators were standing. There can only be one explanation, namely that Levegh, having had the presence of mind to warn the drivers behind him just fractions of a second earlier, was left with virtually no room for overtaking and crashed into the rear-end of Macklin's car in an attempt to get past Macklin's car on the left. The assumption that Macklin's car received a hard blow is confirmed by the fact that the car, which was obviously no longer controllable, was deflected from its original course and, as already described, zigzagged across the track twice, completely out of control.

First and foremost, therefore, Herr Macklin should be asked to describe the situation during the last few seconds.

From where we were standing, he was on the far left. We were, however, unable to see whether the dark-green car blocked his way to such an extent that he had to slam on the brakes. Herr Macklin will presumably confirm what other witnesses have reported, namely that in an attempt to turn right into the pits, Herr Hawthorn's car started skidding and blocked Macklin's passage.

We also saw that Herr Hawthorn was shown the STOP sign twice but he must have overlooked it for some reason or did not want to see it. We assume that he had forgotten the STOP signs during his very fierce battle with Fangio and suddenly remembered the necessity of coming into the pits. At any rate, he slowed down far too late, and the length of track into the pit lane was too short from that speed.

Another possibility is that Hawthorn, while turning right, noticed – or sensed – that Fangio negotiated the entire group of cars involved in the accident, especially since Fangio had been behind him all the time, and that he braked particularly harshly, thereby reinforcing the skidding of his car which was already shooting along sideways.

\* \* \*

The entire set of questions has now been illuminated from different perspectives; as a result three possibilities emerge and are set out below:

1. The car of Herr Levegh lost its front wheel on the right-hand side.
2. The car of Herr Levegh exploded.
3. Herr Levegh's car crashed into the rear of Herr Macklin's car on which the brakes locked for some unknown reason, thereby decelerating the car strongly and causing Herr Levegh's car to lift off.

The following can be said about the individual possibilities:

1. The investigations carried out by Herr von Korff in Le Mans today have revealed that the front axle suspension is complete. Suspension, hubs and wheels are all still mounted on the car, and the tires are also there in fully inflated condition. The rear axle suspension is complete, too; only the tires were burnt in the fire.

2. For the following reasons, an explosion of the car must be excluded:

   a. It was clear to see that the complete car first lifted off the ground and caught fire only after hitting the ground again a few seconds later.

   b. Every explosion is associated with a detonation which nobody heard.

   c. An explosion would have destroyed the frame and other car elements in a way that would be clearly visible.

However, the frame structure is complete, and the remaining car components do not show any signs of explosive forces, either, i.e. forces which would have to have destroyed the car from inside.

The race management and the hospital in Le Mans have meanwhile been requested to submit a breakdown of fatalities killed by fire and those who were killed by car components. Such a survey has not yet been compiled and will only be available in two weeks' time. Quite generally, however, it can be stated that external signs of fire, e.g. burnt clothes, singed hair, etc. have not yet been detected to date.

The most significant proof is probably the corpse of driver Levegh. Secretary Acat from the Automobile Club de l'Ouest was able to identify Herr Levegh only because his corpse did not show any external signs of injury. Herr Levegh was wearing his white woolen sweater and his white pair of trousers. The safety helmet of Herr Levegh, which was handed over to me, still shows its light-red color with just a few minor scratches. An explosion would primarily have torn Herr Levegh's body apart, but this was not the case.

The remaining reports also speak against an explosion; witnesses referred to limbs and mutilated corpses but never to burnt human body parts.

* * *

Orders were given to have the car of driver Macklin with start no. 26 confiscated by the Le Mans police just like our car which will only be released by the Le Mans police in eight to ten days. Herr von Korff has so far been unable to find out whether this has happened. We will, however, receive a photo of that car from Herr Fangio; the photo shows that the rear wheel tire on the left-hand side is missing, and that the car was ripped open at the back and heavily dented in other areas.

An examination of the car may reveal traces of our car's aluminum color on this light-green car, and presumably, the torn sections will also conclusively prove a crash rather than an explosion.

We will shortly provide photographs of the complete front axle, rear axle and other parts of our car.

Concerning the fire, finally, it has to be stated that the quantity of remaining fuel was very small. The car should have come into the pits for refueling within the next 15 minutes. Having driven for exactly two-and-a-half hours and completed the same number of laps as Kling, the car had 52 liters of fuel left in its tank as we were able to establish with great precision. Only this quantity can have burnt.

* * *

Finally, it should also be taken into account that after the tragedy, driver Hawthorn had a nervous breakdown and a crying fit in his pit. It is also reported that he only climbed back into the car after a fierce dispute with the gentlemen from Jaguar. These scenes would probably not have taken place had Herr Hawthorn felt innocent. It is, by contrast, understandable that he was urged to continue the race to demonstrate that he had had nothing to do with the accident.

Untertürkheim, June 14, 1955                    (Neubauer)
Nb/Re

P.S. The following information has just been received:

Herr Acat, Secretary General of the Automobile Club, confirmed that practically nobody had died of burns. All the injuries were inflicted by car parts flying around.

The car of Herr Macklin was confiscated by the police, and it will be examined whether traces of aluminum color are to be found at the rear end of this car.

D.O.

*(Translation of speech by Dr. Könecke. Translator's note: the German –
1950s – style is slightly ponderous, and no attempt was made to translate
this into 'modern' English)*

## Press conference on June 15, 1955

Remarks by Dr. Fritz Könecke, chairman of the Board of
Management of Daimler-Benz AG

### Gentlemen,

We have come together here in Untertürkheim because
of a deeply distressing tragedy.

We mourn the numerous victims of the terrible
accident in Le Mans and our thoughts are with their
families on whom unspeakable pain was inflicted by a
relentless fate.

Daimler-Benz too has been severely struck by this
terrible incident. We mourn the death of a man whom
we were proud to call one of us. His bravery and selfless
comradeship will secure him an honorable place in
motor sport history for all time.

We bow our heads as a sign of respect for the victims
of Le Mans, and we offer our heartfelt condolences to
their bereaved families.

Gentlemen, I would like to thank you most cordially
for accepting our invitation and not sparing the trouble
of a long journey. We have invited you to explain, in all
breadth and clarity, our company's point of view with
regard to this incident which moved people all over the
world.

We decided to convene this conference because we
want to inform you, and thus the public, about the
results of our most scrupulous investigation, and because

we would like to list the preconditions once again which in our opinion have to be fulfilled to prevent accidents on this scale in the future.

To start with, I would like to point out that we started into this arduous race as well prepared in every respect as into any other. The investigation we conducted in all conscientiousness revealed that the accident can on no account be attributed to failure on our part, be that in terms of design, vehicle engineering, driving or race organization. We have sufficient proof to substantiate this statement at any time.

After the accident, the organizers and persons responsible for the race decided to continue the race. The battle of engines was indeed continued and, according to the information available to us, no protest was filed by the highest-ranking French authority.

The executives of our company who were in Le Mans immediately offered to withdraw our cars. However, their attention was drawn to the risk of the access roads becoming overloaded, something that had to be expected in view of the spectators' excitement. This would have jeopardized the rescue operations, i.e. taking the unfortunate victims away and attending to the injured.

It was only in the late evening, first from radio reports and later on in phone calls, that my colleague Nallinger and I myself were informed about this terrible accident and the extent of it. Both ourselves and our executives in Le Mans had for a long time tried to contact each other but had failed due to the telephone network being overloaded. Once the contact had been established and we had been informed about the facts, we immediately gave instructions to take our two well-placed cars with the driver teams Fangio/Moss and Kling/Simon out of the race.

In the course of these discussions, we were confronted with different counter-arguments, especially by the motor sport authorities, but we nevertheless held on to the fundamental decision we had taken and merely postponed our withdrawal to a point in time at which this would no longer jeopardize the rescue operations.

In taking this decision, we were exclusively guided by the feeling of compassion and, notwithstanding our sporting ambitions, by the determination not to score victory on a track on which death had taken such a heavy toll.

We still consider this decision to be right; we would take it again in a similar situation, and we see ourselves reassured one hundred percent by the response of German and foreign press and radio commentaries.

Our cars therefore withdrew from the race at 1:45 hours, and this was announced to the spectators in an official statement by the directorate of Daimler-Benz AG via the speakers. This statement read as follows:

"After talks with the general managers in Stuttgart over the phone and consultations with the chairman of the Board of Management, Dr. Könecke, the representatives of Mercedes-Benz in Le Mans were given instructions to withdraw the company's cars from the race. This decision was taken by Mercedes-Benz as a sign of our deeply felt mourning of the tragedy in Le Mans. Dr. Könecke and the other members of the Board of Management share the grief of the bereaved families and assure them of their heartfelt sympathy."

As soon as this was technically possible, on early Sunday morning, we also sent a telegram to the organizers, asking them to pass the content on to all the parties they considered to be appropriate recipients. This telegram read as follows:

*"At the greatest and most difficult international long-distance race in Le Mans, an accident happened which in its tragic dimensions is the most severe in racing history. This accident also affected us at Daimler-Benz AG.*

*"We would like to express our heartfelt condolences to you and the entire French people. Out of our deepest sympathy for the victims of the accident and the tragic fate of French driver Pierre Levegh, who was a member of our racing team, we decided to withdraw our two cars which were still racing. To prevent a disorganized departure of the spectators, which would have hindered the transport of the wounded to the hospital, we delayed the withdrawal by several hours after permanent consultations with our staff at the racetrack. We kindly ask you to pass on the content of this telegram and our condolences to the parties that appear to be appropriate to you."*

On Monday morning, finally, we started reconstructing the terrible accident with the help of eye witnesses in Le Mans. This reconstruction clearly reveals that we are not responsible for, leave alone guilty of, the accident even though it was one of our racing cars which caused the disaster.

We fully agree with the public when it calls for a clarification of what happened, as well as for precautionary measures to prevent such disasters in the future, even though we have no intention of glossing

over the unavoidable risks which are involved in motor
sport.

We already expressed our own demands in a telegram
we sent to the Sporting Commission of the Fédération
Internationale de l'Automobile, the content of which
your are familiar with. I would like to summarize its
content briefly here:

a. More stringent examination of the suitability of a
   racetrack by the organizers.
b. Improved and fully effective safety measures along the
   track itself.
c. Adequate monitoring of the discipline of all competing
   drivers in keeping with its own demands, and the
   readiness to take even the harshest steps immediately.

In participating in motor sport competitions and in
keeping with the tradition of our company, we have to
date been guided by a sporting spirit and the awareness
that the arduous testing of cars on the racetrack can be
used to good advantage in the technical development of
our production cars.

However, we are not prepared to subordinate our respect
for human life and the awareness that there are limits to
human adequacy in technical development to our sporting
ambitions and our endeavors to achieve technical progress.
Our decision not to compete in Grand Prix racing in 1956
was taken quite some time ago. In addition, we seriously
investigate the question whether we should withdraw
from the remaining Grand Prix races this year already if
the parties responsible do not fulfil the demands I
mentioned to the extent to which this is humanly possible.

The question of future participation in sports car racing is also being scrupulously examined by us; the decision will depend on the measures taken to protect the lives of the spectators.

Before I hand over to my colleague Dr. Nallinger for a report on the race, we will show you original footage of the accident in Le Mans.

After the remarks by Dr. Nallinger, we will be available to answer all your questions, together with all the eye witnesses from our company, who were in Le Mans as drivers, technical staff or spectators. These are Messrs. Fangio, Uhlenhaut, Neubauer, Hundt and Keser, and not least a young Indian gentlemen who took informative photos which you will also be able to see.

In addition to expressing our deeply felt compassion for the victims of this accident, we would like to assure you that our future decisions will solely be guided by humanitarian considerations, by a spirit of sportsmanship and international fairness in competition.

*Chapter 14*

# THE AIR BRAKE CONTROVERSY

In practice for Le Mans in 1952, Mercedes experimented with an air brake that rose up at the rear of the coupé top. Although the air brake was not used for the race that year, the idea re-appeared on the 300SLR for Le Mans in 1955 with a full-width flap behind the open cockpit. The scrutineers asked for the window area to be doubled to the regulations for the rear window of a saloon car at 84 square inches.

Harry Mundy, the expert technical editor of *The Autocar* who would work with Lotus and later Coventry Climax on engine design, investigated the air brake which appeared only on the 300SLR for a few races that summer. Mercedes were yet to use disc brakes and suffered problems with their drum brakes grabbing and cracking drums with the sudden heat from application at high speed. The use of the oil-squirt to counter grabbing was a basic answer to an urgent question, but the air brake was aimed at reducing top speed before using the regular brakes.

"The method of operation on the Mercedes is to hinge upwards the top panel of the tail and the driver's headrest. It is hinged at two points and controlled by two hydraulic rams operated from an engine-driven oil pump. Time taken to raise it is between two and three seconds and, of course, its effect is progressive as a gradually increasing area is available. Operation is by a flick lever situated on the dash, which operates a two-position selector valve. When the cars first appeared at scrutineering, the gear selector mechanism was equipped with an override control which automatically lowered the flap on selection of second gear.

"The drivers had not seen or tried the new automatic device until the cars arrived at Le Mans, but it was quickly decided to remove it from the gear selector, as they preferred to have the operation under their own control at all times.

"There was a considerable variation in the use of the air brake by the different drivers. Kling and Fitch raised the flap at the approach to the pit area and lowered it before entering the curve under the Dunlop Bridge, whereas Fangio and Moss delayed its application until towards the end of the pit area, and took the corner before lowering. Similarly, approaching Mulsanne Corner, Moss and Fangio delayed application until the 300-metre post, lowering after completion of the corner, whereas the other Mercedes drivers brought it into operation at about 475 metres and negotiated the corner with the flap in the lowered position.

"With an area of approximately 7.0sq ft, this air brake should give a retardation of somewhere between minus 0.3 and 0.2g in the higher speed range. It is a great pity that we were unable to see whether or not this interesting device had the desired effect of saving the mechanical brakes.

"Controversy has risen on the grounds that the air brake affects the handling of the car by reducing the weight on the front wheels in its raised position, but this was not necessarily so. By providing the inside of the flap with a concave form and arresting it at a calculated distance from the vertical, the resultant wind forces from the centre of pressure can be arranged to pass through the centre of gravity of the car. In this way any moments tending to lift the front wheels are eliminated. This is, presumably, the method used in the Mercedes; we learned in conversation with Moss and Fitch that neither was able to detect any difference in handling properties, over the wide speed range in which the brake was used.

"Had the Mercedes not withdrawn before the heavy rain came during Sunday, we may have seen whether the air brake achieved the advantage which it appears to have in the wet."

There was a general impression that the use of the air brakes would cause an upset in aerodynamics that would unsettle other cars but John Cooper did several laps of practice in his Cooper sports car and reported being passed by Moss on the approach to Mulsanne as he was applying the air brake. "He reported that he felt no effect on the handling of his very light car."

Mundy pointed out that fears had been expressed about the danger to following cars with less efficient braking than the Mercedes. "But this also applied in 1953 and 1954 when the Dunlop disc brakes were available only to the Jaguar cars. It was one of the highlights in the early part of the 1954 race to see Moss overtaken on the Mulsanne Straight by the 4.9-litre Ferrari of Gonzalez, only to pass him again before the Mulsanne Corner by being able to brake inside."

A similar state of affairs existed among the small cars in 1955 where the lightweight Lotus with its Girling discs, was run into from behind by a Porsche which lacked such good stopping power.

*Chapter 15*

# BACK TO BUSINESS: RACING GOES ON IN HOLLAND

The Dutch Grand Prix at Zandvoort was scheduled the weekend after the tragedy at Le Mans and it went ahead when several other races had cancelled. The Mercedes management was understandably cautious about racing again so soon after their high profile involvement in the accident and their savaging by some sections of the international press. Even the august *Autocar* felt obliged to make mention of "the ruthless purposefulness of the Mercedes-Benz organisation from Germany; a purposefulness that commands admiration and yet stimulates resentment ..."

Dr Fritz Könecke, Chairman of the Board, wrote to Dr. Fritz Nallinger, the board representative in charge of the racing division, to say that he had deep reservations about the company taking part in the Grand Prix in Holland. "Even if we convince ourselves in the time available that the circuit is not dangerous and even if there is no accident, which I have reason to believe will be the case, the public will have doubts about our taking part because they believe that, at such short notice, we will be unable to fulfil our declaration that in future we will not appear where safety is in doubt.

"I fear a negative response – even if all goes well – and I believe that, rather than jeopardise our credibility with the public, we should reduce our team's chances for the rest of the Grand Prix season, and that includes the drivers' chances of the world title. Personally, I would rather see financial compensation for the drivers for any possible losses of prize money that may result."

Nallinger did not agree, feeling that the team's decision to withdraw and not race in Holland would be taken as tacit admission of responsibility for the terrible events at Le Mans.

If there was nervousness at Mercedes's domination of Grand Prix racing, *Autocar* could recognise the polished professionalism of the German team at Zandvoort: "At 1pm precisely the three silver Mercedes cars were wheeled out and lined up *en echelon* by the pit. They were spotless; their race numbers were beautifully inscribed in red, outlined with black; each car had its team of mechanics. Herr Neubauer came out on to the circuit, green label in wide-brimmed hat, neatly suited in brown. His chair was handed over the counter; two stopwatches hung round his neck. At 1.15pm senior mechanics sat in the cars; the bonnets came off and warming-up began, various parts of the engine being felt by hand for temperature rise. They were warmed up at even revolutions – not for a long time was blipping permitted. Tyre temperatures were methodically checked; khaki sheets then draped the engines. At 1.50pm each car was wheeled backwards alongside the starting grid, and when they took up station in the front row (Fangio, Moss and Kling) you could imagine Neubauer saying 'Right – now let's get down to business ...'"

The GPs of Switzerland and Spain had been cancelled and it was expected that the French race would be either cancelled or postponed.

The Dutch, having suffered under German occupation during the war, were secretly amused that their circuit had been formed in 1942 with the encouragement and assistance of the German army under the guise of a training ground with access roads, when in fact they were laying the foundations for a post-war racing circuit.

John Fitch was once again listed as a Mercedes reserve team driver but the American was not comfortable with car or circuit and was well adrift of the team times with a best lap of 1min 48.3sec that was a full 5sec slower than engineer Uhlenhaut's time.

For the first time that season the silver arrows filled the front row with Fangio on pole, Moss and then Kling. Luigi Musso had sparked respect with the 250F Maserati setting a time just 0.1sec slower than Kling's Mercedes. Hawthorn was beside him on the second row with the Ferrari with a time equalled later by Jean Behra's Maserati.

The race itself was another tutorial for Moss, following in the wheel tracks of Fangio. Musso in the works 250F had sparked from the start to follow Fangio from the grid but Moss soon established the 1–2 domination. Kling slid off the circuit while disputing fifth with the Maseratis of Behra and Mières.

In the latter stages of the race, Moss was showing travel stains of oil grime and he finished black-faced and trailing oil smoke in the closing laps. He was paying the penalty of his close attention to racing in Fangio's wheel tracks. Post race checks showed that Fangio's engine was clean; Moss's was full of sand. The engineering team, including Uhlenhaut, power unit engineer Lamm, and Kosteletzky, head of the racing workshop, jointly signed a letter to Neubauer asking that he instil team orders on Moss. It was interesting that they felt obliged to combine with their request, presumably feeling safety in numbers against Neubauer's weight in team management.

The letter read: "The inspection of Moss's engine, after oil fouling of one cylinder towards the end of the race, showed that the inlet valves of the rear cylinder block portion were badly damaged. Besides this, cylinders 6, 7 and 8 showed signs of excessive wear which can be traced back only to the large amounts of sand entering the engine.

"May we ask you to alert the drivers to the unacceptability of 'nose-to-tail running' when this is not strictly demanded by racing conditions. This applies especially to particularly dusty or sandy circuits. This instruction must be adhered to at all times for the sake of technical reliability."

A hand-written postscript note from Kosteletzky suggested a tail-gating distance of at least 30–50 metres ...

*Chapter 16*

# BRITON WINS THE
# BRITISH GRAND PRIX

Britain stood firm. The French Government banned all motor racing in the wake of the Le Mans disaster. The Italian Government followed suit, but soon changed its mind. The Swiss would ban motor racing forever and stick by the decision. In Germany the Grand Prix on the old Nürburgring, a circuit designed for the purpose of motor racing had been cancelled because of safety measures but the British Grand Prix on the new Aintree circuit never seemed to be in question with its backing from the staid *Daily Telegraph* and under the stewardship of the august Royal Automobile Club. It was the second Grand Prix to be held since Le Mans, five weeks after the disaster.

Mercedes brought four Monaco-style short-chassis cars with outboard front brakes for Fangio, Moss, Kling and Taruffi, the 48-year-old Italian who was standing in for Herrmann, still recovering from his Monaco injuries. The Moss car had a one-piece front-hinged engine cover. They also had a cockpit lever to adjust the rear torsion bar so that the drivers could re-set the suspension to compensate as the fuel load lightened during the race.

It was the first time the post-war British Grand Prix had been staged at Aintree, where a motor sporting course had been built in and around the famous horse-race track near Liverpool, enjoying the grandstands, restaurants, bars and general facilities for the equine set. It was a luxury setting by motor racing standards. There had been Grand Prix races at Brooklands in the 1920s and races in the late 1930s at Donington Park with Mercedes and Auto-Union entries that deserved Grand Prix titles but never received them. Donington and Brooklands had been swallowed-up during the war and when motor racing finally returned in Britain it was at Silverstone, on the bleak flat airfield circuit where the first post-war British Grand Prix was staged in 1948, when Villoresi won in a Maserati. In 1951 with the Grand Prix as part of the World Championship series, the airfield circuit staged a history-making win when Gonzalez scored the first *Grand Épreuve* victory in one of Enzo Ferrari's cars.

Moss had won races at Aintree in 1954 with his privately owned and entered 250F Maserati which he rented to other drivers in 1955 and raced it when events did not clash with his Mercedes commitments. He held the lap record at 2min 00.6sec and he was immediately at home in the Mercedes, setting the pole position lap at 2min 00.4sec from Fangio (2min 00.6sec) and Behra's Maserati (2min 01.4sec). Kling and Taruffi were on row two with the other pair of silver Mercedes. It is worth noting that Fangio's best lap in the Mercedes equalled Moss's 1954 lap record in the Maserati.

In its second season of Grand Prix racing, the Mercedes team could enjoy the luxury – or the complication – of a driver choice between five different versions of the same

W196 model. There was the streamliner that appeared when Mercedes made its post-war Grand Prix comeback at Reims in 1954 and was seen again, bouncing off the marker drums in the British Grand Prix at Silverstone a few weeks later. The same basic chassis but with open bodywork was entered for the German Grand Prix.

A medium wheelbase chassis with the same inboard brake arrangement was used in Argentina for the start of this 1955 season. For Monaco an ultra-short chassis featured more conventional outboard brakes, mainly because there was nowhere to place them inboard in the shortened chassis. A third version of the W196 with a wheelbase in between the two and using outboard brakes was used for the Belgian Grand Prix at Spa. For Aintree there were two different types of chassis entered. Kling and Taruffi had the medium chassis with outboard brakes. Moss and Fangio had the ultra-short 'Monaco' chassis with the steering box well forward and the steering arms and track rods in front of the wheels. They were also fitted with an over-ride control on the suspension dampers.

Mercedes were going Grand Prix racing in the grand manner, despite the fact that the company had already announced that they would be withdrawing from Grand Prix racing at the end of the season. There was still the suggestion that they might continue in sports car racing, but the Le Mans disaster would presumably have eroded that confidence. It was reckoned that the racing staff in Stuttgart, excluding those responsible for machining and building the cars, numbered a total of 270 which was around twelve times the size of any British team.

Chris Amon, the young New Zealander who would lead the Ferrari team at the end of the 1960s and the Matra team at the beginning of the 1970s, was something of a student of motor racing history, and he wondered who would have been World Champion if Fangio or Moss had not been driving the Mercedes. "As good as it was, the W196 was certainly flattered by its drivers. If Moss or Fangio had been in a works Maserati, the pace of the season would have changed considerably."

In modern terms, it would have been like removing Michael Schumacher from the Ferrari team equation.

Fellow-New Zealander Howden Ganley, former BRM works driver and now a director of the British Racing Drivers' Club has his own observation on the historical what-if situation. "If Fangio and Moss had been in 250F Maseratis in 1955 they would have beaten the W196 Mercedes (an inferior design made to win by superb facilities and two of the best drivers) but Fangio would still have been World Champion. However, if Lancia had enjoyed the same resources as Mercedes, in my opinion the D50 would have been the dominant car."

Peter Collins was on the back row of the grid having suffered engine problems in the 250F Maserati owned by the Owen Organisation as a test bed for the BRM cars. Ironically in view of the previous comments by Chris Amon, this was the actual car he drove to make his name in New Zealand. Last by some measure because of minimal practice in his just-completed car was Jack Brabham, the determined Australian who would be World Champion just four years later. In a Cooper … He was driving a Cooper special he had built himself, confected by stretching a sports car and fitting a Bristol engine in the back. It was supposed that the nominally 2-litre sports car engine had been increased to 2.2-litres, thus qualifying as a Formula 1 power unit, but it was later found that there had not been time for the engine to be increased in capacity and it was always a shade under 2-litres. It had been 'nodded through' by Dean Delamont, competition 'head' of the RAC.

The Ferrari team was not really in contention with their older cars and Castellotti was fastest on the fourth row of the grid. Surprise of practice was the pace of Harry Schell in the new Vanwall, up on row three between the Maseratis of Mières and Simon, but he lost ground with a stall at the start.

An hour before the start, the drivers were taken on a lap of the course, each sitting on the back of an Austin-Healey. It said much for Fangio's adulation and his reputation as champion, that the crowd on the embankment broke through the fences and mobbed his car with programmes waved for autographs.

Moss led away from pole position, but Fangio was in front at the end of the first lap. Moss led again on the 18th lap and the crowd wondered whether this would be his day but Fangio was ahead on lap 26.

*Autosport* columnist Nigel Roebuck was at the race as a little lad, never knowing that he would become top man in his field in Formula 1 and become close friends with the very same Stirling Moss. Roebuck had read the Moss diaries in 2003 and noted in a thoughtful piece in *Motor Sport* that Moss's diary entry for that day, read: *Took lead at start, due to Behra's proximity. Let Fangio lead later, and at 18 laps took the lead to the end.* Roebuck noted the significance of the word *let* ...

The field was decimating itself. Castellotti out with Ferrari transmission problems, Schell's Vanwall out with a broken accelerator pedal, Marr's Connaught spun out at Bechers corner (named after the famous Bechers Brook jump on the steeplechase course) with a fractured brake pipe, Simon out with a broken gear selector in the 250F and gearbox problems for Salvadori in the Gilbey Engineering 250F.

Schell had strolled back to the pits across the infield, swinging his helmet. His Vanwall was out but his race was not over. Ken Wharton had pitted with an engine problem in the second Vanwall but the irrepressible Schell was urging the mechanics to put the matter right and he would take the car back into the race. Never mind that he was some 15 laps behind the leaders. His was the only British car left in the British Grand Prix and Harry was going for it. He caught and passed Castellotti's Ferrari, although several laps behind and they gave the crowd something to cheer about. When Moss and Fangio came by, Schell gave them plenty of room and then settled in behind them, maintaining the pace of the leaders to give an indication of the success to come for Tony Vandervell's green cars. The Wharton/Schell Vanwall was placed ninth, but Schell had proved his point. He would *never* give up.

Harry was born in Paris to American parents who ran a racing team, Ecurie Bleue, with Delahayes and Talbots. They entered René Dreyfus in a Delahaye in a pre-war '500' at Indianapolis and young Harry went along as junior pit crew in the family team. In 1949 he was racing a Talbot and in 1950 he bought a Cooper-JAP running it as a '500' and switching to a 1,100cc JAP for Formula 1. At Monaco in 1950 he raced as a '500' to win his heat in the Formula 3 race and then finished second to Moss in another Cooper-JAP in the final. For the Grand Prix with the bigger engine fitted, Harry started one from last and was one of the first retirements when he was caught up in a multiple crash on the second lap. But he had made history. His Cooper was the first of the marque to start in a *Grand Épreuve*.

With 40 laps to go at Aintree, Moss was 12sec in front but Neubauer was signalling him 'PI'. It was not 'Place One' but *Piano* – gently. Quite why the German team manager used Italian signals is not clear after half a century.

Moss was out in front again in the closing stages and as if to underline his mastery of Aintree, he set a new lap record on the penultimate lap. Would he be allowed to win? Was Fangio under Mercedes orders to let him? Stirling backed off as he approached the chequered flag and waved Fangio through, but Fangio only pulled alongside and Moss won his first *Grand Épreuve*. He was the first British driver to win the British Grand Prix and in a sporting gesture he handed his winner's garland to Fangio after the presentation.

Mercedes finished 1–2–3–4: Moss, Fangio, Kling and Taruffi a lap down. There were only nine finishers. Peter Garnier drew the race and the Mercedes domination into focus in his 'Sport' column in *The Autocar* of 22 July 1955. His sentiment of the racing ceasing to be a spectacle could have been written fifty years later in the era of the dominant Schumacher/Ferrari combination: "Last Saturday's Grand Prix showed, once again, the unassailable superiority of the Mercedes team and one or two people were heard grumbling to Artur Keser, the Mercedes PRO, that Grand Prix racing has ceased to be a spectacle and is just a procession of Mercedes cars with a motor race going on astern. That's just about what it amounts to (though the clockwise regularity of the Mercs never fail to impress), but it is not as though the remainder of the field at Aintree was outclassed in speed alone – the cars were hopelessly outclassed in reliability; twenty-four started and only nine finished. Of the eight Maseratis, two finished; of the three Ferraris and three Gordinis, one of each finished; of the two Vanwalls, one finished and, of the three Connaughts and one Cooper, none completed the course; of the four Mercedes-Benz, all four finished.

"One must, obviously, make allowances for the effects of slower cars attempting to keep up with a race speed set by the leaders that is way beyond their capabilities – bent valves, burned pistons and so on – and the adverse effects of excursions off the circuit. But these factors accounted for, perhaps, seven of the retirements – the remainder were directly attributable to unreliability.

"It seems that a useful lesson can be learned from this. While the Mercedes mechanics were sitting, unemployed, watching their cars, the other pit staffs were kept busy for most of the race ..."

Jack Brabham's retirement late in the race when the engine overheated went un-noticed in the excitement of Stirling's first Grand Prix win and the wondering about whether Fangio had gifted him the race. The Australian had made a sort of history so modest that it had been instantly forgotten but that erudite if quirkily pedantic racing historian Leonard Setright would remember it in his book *The Grand Prix Car* published in 1973: "It (the Bristol-engined Cooper) was the slowest car there; but it was also the first rear-engined Formula 1 car to be raced in an international event since the passing of the days of Auto Union; therefore with Brabham as its driver, it accounted for two straws in the wind ..."

### Leslie Marr's Grand Prix memories

Professional artist and amateur racing driver, Leslie Marr, drove his streamlined Formula 1 Connaught in the 1955 British Grand Prix and 50 years later he recalled that race weekend: "When we set off from our little mews garage in London, a cheerful Cockney, who knew we were going to race in the Grand Prix and that the 'Mercs' would be there, shouted out 'Bring us back a German helmet, mate!' Not very politically correct now, but typical of the humour then.

"We had foolishly booked a hotel on the wrong side of the Mersey and had to negotiate the busy Mersey Tunnel on the morning of the race. The driver of our transporter, an old converted bus, managed to bring all three lanes of traffic to a standstill at an intersection under the river, and an irate policeman had to sort it out. We were now very late and the police, surprisingly after the chaos we had caused in the tunnel, provided an escort to the track with sirens wailing and bells ringing ...

"I had qualified 19th in a field of 25 after fuel injection problems, which I felt was quite reasonable, considering the strength of the field. To my embarrassment, I stalled at the start and had to wait until my mechanics, who had walked some distance up the track to watch the start, had to run all the way back to push me ... The car went well enough and I was working my way through the back markers when suddenly I was braking for a corner and realised I had *no*

*Disaster at Le Mans. The smoking remains of Levegh's wrecked Mercedes 300SLR after it had cannoned off the back of Macklin's Austin-Healey and hurdled the spectator bank. Levegh and more than 80 spectators were killed. Spectators soon crowded back into the area with blood still staining the ground. (LAT)*

*The damaged rear quarter of Lance Macklin's Austin-Healey 100S after Levegh's Mercedes-Benz had ridden into the back of it, triggering the huge accident. The Healey slammed back and forth across the track but Macklin was unharmed. (Bill Piggott Collection)*

*Factory archive photograph of the 300SLR Mercedes in Le Mans trim with the air-brake flap raised. (DaimlerChrysler Archive)*

*Fangio leads Moss in the Dutch Grand Prix at Zandvoort in a shot typical of the 1955 season. Stirling was warned by the team engineers for driving too close to Fangio. His car was smoking in the closing stages and a post-race check revealed that while Fangio's engine was clean, Moss's power plant was choked with sand thrown up in Fangio's slipstream. (David Hodges Collection)*

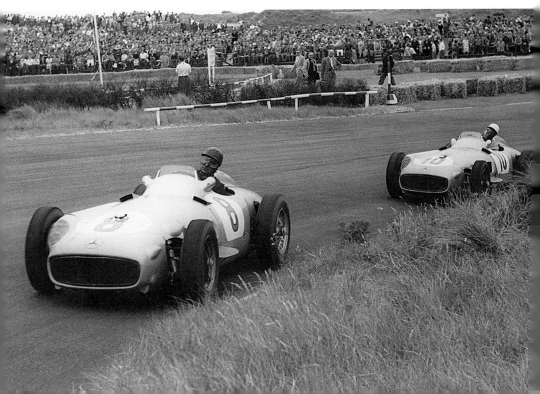

The chequered flag for another Fangio-Moss 1–2 for Mercedes-Benz at Zandvoort. The race was run the weekend following the tragedy at Le Mans and Mercedes were criticised inside and outside the company for apparent lack of respect. (David Hodges Collection)

The start of the first British Grand Prix to be held on the Aintree circuit, built in and around the famous horse-racing venue, held five weeks after the Le Mans accident. Motor racing had been banned in France, Italy, Switzerland and Germany. Fangio holds a slender lead from Moss off the line with Karl Kling and Piero Taruffi following in the other Mercedes works team cars. (LAT)

*Stirling Moss was the crowd's hero at Aintree that afternoon in 1955, proudly sporting the Union Jack behind his head in the W196 Mercedes-Benz – the epitome of German motorsport engineering. The war had been over for barely a decade.* (LAT)

*Fangio leads but Moss would head more laps of his 'home' race than he had at any event earlier in the season. His win was said to be because Fangio had driven to team orders, but this would always be a matter of conjecture.* (David Hodges Collection)

*Stirling Moss, goggle-grimed, weary but elated after winning his home race – and the first World Championship Grand Prix of his career. In a decade of Formula 1 he would go on to win a total of 16 GPs and 16 pole positions.* (LAT)

*At Aintree Mercedes-Benz achieved a commanding 1–2–3–4 result, and the team drivers were taken on a parade lap of the circuit in Austin-Healey sports cars. From left: engineer Rudi Uhlenhaut, Juan Manuel Fangio, Piero Taruffi, Stirling Moss, Karl Kling and team manager Alfred Neubauer.* (DaimlerChrysler Archive)

Above: *Stirling Moss accelerates away from the pits in the 1955 Swedish Grand Prix on the Kristianstadt circuit, a purpose-built 4-mile course laid out on the country property of a friend of the Swedish Prince Berthil. Fangio and Moss finished an untroubled 1–2.* (DaimlerChrysler Archive)

Left: *Fangio leads Moss in the 300SLR Mercedes to totally dominate the slender field in the Swedish Grand Prix.* (LAT)

Above right: *Moss follows Fangio under the pedestrian bridge on the Kristianstadt circuit. Late in the race Moss was hit by a stone that smashed his goggles, and a surgeon had to remove splinters from his left eye after the race.* (DaimlerChrysler Archive)

Right: *The final Grand Prix of the 1955 season was the Italian at Monza. The race was held for the first time on a 10km (6.2-mile) circuit that combined the new bankings as well as the road course. The circuit was originally built in 1922 with bankings but these were demolished in 1939. This Mercedes-dominated view shows Fangio, Taruffi and Kling on the road circuit with Hawthorn (Ferrari) and Moss on the banking – spectators at the start/finish could see the cars twice a lap.* (David Hodges Collection)

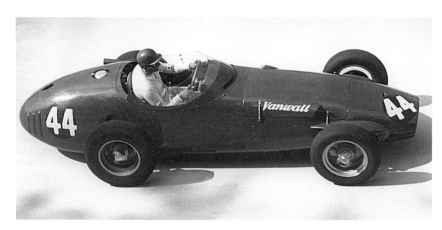

Above left: *Ken Wharton drove an unspectacular race in a Vanwall at Monza, qualifying 17th and retiring with broken fuel injection. Harry Schell qualified 13th in the other Vanwall and was a retirement after seven laps when the rear suspension collapsed on the rough banked section.* (David Hodges Collection)

Left: *Fangio swooping across the banking to win the 1955 Italian Grand Prix in the streamlined Mercedes-Benz W196. The team had covered their bets on the fast circuit with streamlined cars for Fangio and Moss and open-wheelers for Kling and Taruffi. Moss suffered a smashed windscreen and a pit stop, eventually retiring with fastest lap and a driveshaft failure. Fangio and Taruffi finished 1–2.* (DaimlerChrysler Archive)

Above: *Piero Taruffi finished second to Fangio in his 'home' Italian Grand Prix at Monza, perhaps hoping team manager Neubauer would give him the 'nod' and let him win as he had supposedly done with Moss at Aintree, but this never happened.* (LAT)

Right: *Fangio and Moss led early in the Italian Grand Prix, gathering speed advantage from the streamlined bodies on the steep but uneven bankings being used for the first time in post-war years at Monza. They were popular with spectators; not with drivers.* (David Hodges Collection)

*Mercedes-Benz dominated the 1955 season by their attention to detail engineering, regarded as normal half a century later but the full-size aerodynamic testing with the driver at the wheel was pioneering stuff. (David Hodges Collection)*

*Stirling Moss racing to win the crash-marred 1955 Tourist Trophy at Dundrod in Northern Ireland. His right-rear tyre had thrown a tread and he had slammed the bank at Wheeler's Corner, damaging the bodywork in most un-Moss-like fashion. (Geoff Goddard)*

*Fangio leading the singleton works D-type Jaguar of Mike Hawthorn, who took the battle to the Mercedes team and would probably have been second but for a late-race 'off'. Fangio finished second, sharing with Karl Kling.* (LAT)

*Jean Behra in the works Maserati heading Jacques Swaters in the yellow Ecurie National Belge Ferrari. This was the race where Behra crashed and overturned the Maserati, suffering broken bones and the loss of his left ear.* (David Hodges Collection)

Left: *Birthday treat for Stirling Moss. He took the chequered flag at Dundrod, winning the Tourist Trophy race in his battered Mercedes. His mother baked a cake for his 26th birthday, decked out with a silver Mercedes star.* (DaimlerChrysler Archive)

Below left: *Winning TT duo: Stirling Moss and his American team-mate John Fitch in laurel wreaths. Their win put Mercedes back in with a chance of winning the World Sports Car Championship.* (LAT)

Right: *A movie legend died when James Dean was killed at the wheel of the silver Porsche 550 Spyder that he nicknamed* The Little Bastard. *Dean, seen here with his 356 Speedster, was in his race car en route to a race in California when he collided with a 1938 Ford making a turn at an intersection.* (Pictorial Press)

Below: *Things seemed to run in threes for Dean, who was 26 when he died. He had starred in three major movies –* Rebel Without a Cause, East of Eden *and* Giant *– and he had competed in three sports car races.* (Pictorial Press)

Jack Brabham won the 1955 Australian Grand Prix in what was effectively the first Brabham-built car. He had concocted a recipe for success by effectively reminding Cooper of their recent heritage and converting the front-engined Cooper-Bristol so that the engine was in the rear. It was not a thing of beauty but it served the purpose and gave Brabham his first Grand Prix victory. (Paul Cross Collection)

The Moss/Collins 300SLR would survive two accidents and still win the Targa Florio and the Sports Car Championship – by just one point – on the 45-mile mountain course in Sicily. Peter Collins is seen at the wheel, on his first drive for Mercedes … and this was Stirling Moss's last! It was also the last appearance of the works Mercedes team in the 1950s. (David Hodges Collection)

Stirling Moss led the first four laps of the Targa Florio but then spun off the road and down into a field, where the 300SLR had to be pushed out by an enthusiastic army of Sicilian spectators. He pits here for a damage check and for Collins to take over. (DaimlerChrysler Archive)

Eugenio Castellotti in the works Ferrari snatched the lead in the 1955 Targa Florio when Moss spun his Mercedes 300SLR off the road while leading. Castellotti finished third in the Ferrari behind the Mercedes cars of Moss and Fangio, and ahead of the Titterington/Fitch 300SLR. There were no flag marshals on the 45-mile course – spectator safety seemed to be down to personal choice. (LAT)

*Tony Brooks in the Connaught on his way to winning the Syracuse Grand Prix at the end of October 1955 – and becoming the first British driver to win a foreign Grand Prix since Segrave won the San Sebastian Grand Prix in 1924! It was his first drive in a Grand Prix car, having only begun racing three years earlier. He had chosen dentistry as a career and was studying dental textbooks on the flight to Syracuse. He was 23.* (David Hodges Collection)

*A 300SLR GT, one of two closed versions of the 300SLR built for the subsequently cancelled 1955 Carrera PanAmericana, was used by engineer Rudi Uhlenhaut as his own personal transport.* (DaimlerChrysler Archive)

*brakes at all*. I pushed the pedal harder but the car spun and ran backwards into a ploughed field. I was lucky that it stayed right side up because there were no seat-belts or roll bars then. Just before this, I had spotted a car close behind me in the mirrors and, thinking it was Tony Rolt in another Connaught, had waved him past. This gave rise to a report in one of the newspapers that 'Marr had gone well, but retired owing to an excess of politeness ...'

"I tried to get some spectators to push the car out and get me started again, but without success, so I walked back to the beer tent where there were quite a few drivers who had retired and were drowning their misfortunes. In fact when we inspected the car later, we realised that I had had a lucky escape. We had just started using discs and as we had no previous experience, it was a case of trial and error.

"We didn't know that the front discs were getting red hot and boiling the fluid, which meant no front brakes and one pushed the pedal harder and locked the rears, which in turn caused the car to spin and somersault. This had happened to two other Connaughts in earlier races and it would have happened to me, but for that soft ploughed field ..."

*Chapter 17*

# SWEDISH MIXTURE
# AS BEFORE

The Swedish Grand Prix on the Kristianstad circuit in southern Sweden was for sports cars and was the first Grand Prix to carry the title in Sweden since the 1930s. Prince Bertil of Sweden was a Vice President of the FIA and anxious for a race to be held in his country which could perhaps lead to a fully-fledged Grand Prix. The problem was how and where to run a race since, like Britain, public roads were not allowed to be used for racing. Prince Bertil solved the problem by persuading a wealthy friend to create a four-mile racing circuit on his property at Kristianstad.

The entry made up in quality what it lacked in size. There were Mercedes 300SLRs for Fangio and Moss, a Ferrari for Castellotti, two Maseratis for Behra and Benoit Musy, and two works Aston Martins for Collins and Roy Salvadori. The only Jaguar, Duncan Hamilton's privately entered D-type, would be raced by Michael Head, whose son Patrick would later continue the family name and fame in motorsport, heading the technical side of the Williams Grand Prix team.

As a measure of what might have been but for the cancellation of the German Grand Prix, Mercedes had been testing on the 14.5-mile Nürburgring prior to the sports car race in Sweden and Moss set an unofficial lap record of 9min 39.7sec (87.99mph/141.56kph) in the 2.5-litre 290bhp W196. This compared with Herrmann Lang's record lap in 1939 at 9min 43.1sec (87.37mph/140.58) in the supercharged 3-litre, 485bhp pre-war Mercedes.

Wolfgang von Trips had been invited along as a member of the Mercedes group, to gain experience working with the team and driving a 300SL in a supporting race. Neubauer felt it was important for Trips to be involved. The factory had sent three competition versions of the production 300SL to Sweden for Trips and two local drivers. Trips was asked to drive one car back to Germany but the local dealer was on holiday so he suggested Trips spend a few days touring Sweden. He took Denis Jenkinson with him. 'Jenks' had met von Trips on the 1955 Mille Miglia when the German driver was competing in his own privately-entered 1,300cc Porsche.

The Mercedes team were totally dominant in the race. Fangio was on pole after two days of practice with Moss in his shadow, a full five seconds faster than Castellotti's 4.4-litre Ferrari. The race was a runaway procession for Mercedes. Salvadori's Aston Martin was lapped by Fangio and Moss on the 12th lap and Head's Jaguar was lapped on the 13th tour.

Late in the race, Moss was hit by a stone, smashing his goggles. "At the end of the race," he recalled, "blood was running down my face. Immediately after the finish I went to hospital where a surgeon picked splinters out of my left eye."

Michael Head was best placed British driver in a British car, finishing 6th, two laps behind the Mercedes pair.

Col Michael William Henry Head, RA, was born in Birr, Ireland, in 1912. He joined the army and from 1949 to 1951 he was assistant British Military Attaché in the Scandinavian countries which led to his enthusiasm for racing his Jaguars there. He had started racing in club events at Donington and Brooklands in an SS, and in 1939 he was a member of the Army motorcycle team in the International Six Days Trial in Austria. He also competed in motorcycle scrambling which is presumably where son Patrick would gather his enthusiasm for motorcycles. In 1952 Head drove his white XK120 to win in Helsinki and in 1954 he won the same race again, going on to the Lappeen races and winning there on a dirt circuit. On his way home he won a 50-mile sports car race at Hedemora in Sweden.

The GT race at Kristianstad in 1955 for cars over 2-litres was another 1–2 for Mercedes, Trips having led for much of the race but obediently falling in behind Kling's 300SL.

The race for 500cc cars, described in the programme as 'Midgets' was dominated by the Frenchman, André Loens, in a Cooper Norton but the start had been robustly contested and that quintessential Englishman, Ken Tyrrell, disputed the lead in the first two laps before retirement. In fact Tyrrell had set pole position in practice and would take fastest race lap. The following weekend, still in Sweden, Tyrrell would win at Karlskoga ahead of a top field. Tyrrell's performance in those races had gathered the attention of Aston Martin team manager, John Wyer, and he was offered a works test at Goodwood. Ken would later say that he was testing for the number six seat in the team, but this became number seven and surplus to team requirements when Stirling Moss became available following the withdrawal of Mercedes at the end of the 1955 summer.

Rudolf Uhlenhaut had driven up from Stuttgart in his very special coupé version of the 300SLR, one of only two built, and considered his personal ultimate transport now that the South American race for which they had been created, had been cancelled. Denis Jenkinson fiercely defended his independence as a journalist, but he was regarded, and probably regarded himself, as an honorary member of the Mercedes team after the win in the Mille Miglia when he rode alongside Moss. Uhlenhaut offered him a ride to the circuit in the special coupé and while the layout of the cockpit was identical to their open Mille Miglia car, the coupé body retained the noise that had been blown away on the 1,000-mile race round Italy. He would write in *Motor Sport*: "The noise inside the coupé body was out of all proportion, the mechanical thrashing that came from the engine being due to everything running on roller bearings, and the central drive to the camshafts, magnetos, dynamo and injection pump being an enormous train of tiny gear-wheels. For just a few miles I was once more able to thrill to the exciting acceleration in bottom and second gear, as the tachometer whistled around from 2,500 to 6,000 almost as quickly as you could follow it. Although we only needed to use the bottom two gears of the five-speed box, we were soon in the paddock, but even that short time convinced me once more that these SLR motorcars are a fantastic step forward in automobile engineering."

*Chapter 18*

# BANKING
# ON MONZA

The Italian Grand Prix on the Monza *Autodromo* in the Royal Park northeast of Milan took on a new and controversial look for 1955 with the completion of the new banked track. This was incorporated with the existing road course to provide a total length of 10 kilometres (6.215 miles) – exactly the same overall as the original track, also built with a banking in 1922. In 1939 this banked section had been demolished and after the ravages of war, racing eventually returned to Monza in 1948 and the new banked track would be built to mirror Indianapolis, mainly to attract American entries.

It seemed that the new track layout appealed only to the public. While the drivers had major reservations, the public in the grandstands opposite the pits could see the cars twice a lap, weirdly coming off the banking as well as threading out of the road course running in parallel.

The revised track was opened for testing in August, six weeks before the Grand Prix and Mercedes brought five streamlined and two open-wheeled Grand Prix cars along with engineer Uhlenhaut's 300SLR.

Tests included an air-brake panel on the tail along the lines of the system used at Le Mans, but it produced more problems of instability than advantages under braking and was not used for the race. Mercedes had commissioned special tyres from Continental to cope with the high speeds on the banking, while the D50 Lancias being entered for the first time by Scuderia Ferrari for Castellotti, Farina and Villoresi, suffered so badly with tyres bursting in practice that the cars were withdrawn and Ferrari resorted to a singleton ageing Super Squalo for Castellotti.

Mercedes had brought seven cars for four drivers but Ferrari had brought *nine* – including the four D50 Lancias – for six drivers. The chaotic tyre situation that manifested itself with high-speed incidents meant that eventually Farina and Villoresi would be stood down for the race after qualifying and fate would decree that Farina, the first World Champion in 1950, would never race again. He was one of the Italian 'old guard' having started his career in a 1932 hill climb and graduating to a place in the Alfa Romeo team where Tazio Nuvolari was his mentor, teaching him the finer points of winning against the great odds of the German teams in the late 1930s. The war stole his best years but he came back winning with a Maserati and when Alfa Romeo returned he was once again a works driver.

It was always reckoned that Moss modelled himself on Farina's imperious straight-arm style behind the wheel, but Stirling discounted this in *All But My Life* written in 1963 with Ken Purdy. "I copied Farina's posture, his attitude at the wheel and you'll hear it said that I did this because I knew the straight-arm position was efficient.

Nonsense. I didn't know anything of that kind. I took it over because I liked the way it looked. One looked better, driving that way. I didn't *like* it at all. It felt strange, awkward. But I kept on until in the end I got to the stage where I honestly did like it ..."

Farina's last win was in the 1953 German GP in a Ferrari and he was sidelined with injuries during 1954 and into 1955. Like Mike Hawthorn, Farina was a World Champion who met his death on the public road, driving a Lotus Cortina in 1966.

For the race Mercedes entered streamlined cars for Fangio and Moss and open-wheelers for Kling and Piero Taruffi, the latter having his second Mercedes drive for the season, selected as the Italian 'guest' driver in his home race.

Qualifying saw Mercedes in command with Fangio and Moss in the streamliners with Kling beside them on the front row. Castellotti's old Ferrari was on the second row with a gap beside him where Farina's Lancia had qualified before withdrawal on race morning. Musso was on the third row with the semi-streamlined Maserati beside Mières in a regular open-wheeled 250F Maserati with a gap where Villoresi's Lancia would have been. Taruffi was on row four with the Mercedes beside Musso's Maserati. Collins (Maserati), Maglioli (Ferrari) and Schell (Vanwall) were on row five. Hawthorn and Trintignant were back on row six with the dusted-off Super Squalo Ferraris with longer tails and a revised air intake.

The four Mercedes took early command of the race to the surprise of none but the most fanatical *tifosi*, running Fangio–Moss–Taruffi–Kling but the uneven bankings caused a variety of problems. Schell retired on the seventh lap with the Vanwall's rear suspension collapsed. Kling popped up a new lap record at 131.3mph (211.3kph) and then Moss was peeling off for the pits with a smashed windscreen, perhaps a legacy of the close station he was holding on Fangio, regardless of the management's warning after Zandvoort and his smashed goggles in Sweden. Mercedes had a replacement screen waiting and Moss rejoined in eighth place now driving at his own pace and urging his Mercedes to new lap records with a best of 134mph (215.6kph) but then a driveshaft failed and Stirling was a retirement. Kling had been a secure second behind Fangio and ahead of Taruffi but on lap 33 the German driver pulled over and rolled to a halt with a broken prop shaft, a fault traced to an assembly failure. Fangio and Taruffi were now well out in the lead running one–two.

Taruffi might have been hoping for the Neubauer nod that would slow Fangio and give him the race on his home track, as had happened with Kling in Germany and Moss in Britain, but the nod never came and the pair finished half a second apart with the Silver Fox second in the Silver Arrow having driven an exemplary race. Castellotti was third for Ferrari with Behra fourth in the Maserati and the rest of the field well adrift.

Taruffi was a thinking man's racing driver, an engineer who had designed and built his own quaint 'Tarf' cars, twin-boom devices with the engine in one pod and the driver in the other. He was more at home in sports cars and in fact his first race was in the 1930 Mille Miglia. He was just short of 50-years-old when he drove the Mercedes to second place at Monza.

Moss had a high regard for his abilities: "Piero was an

example of a particularly intelligent man in motor racing. He was never in the very first rank, but he certainly did do a great deal of motor racing. Most people watching motor racing don't appreciate Taruffi's kind of intelligence. If a bloke goes into a corner five miles an hour too fast and manages to get around somehow, all crossed up but still gets around, he's not brave, he's stupid. Taruffi was a good driver in sports cars and he knew it and he knew that on his day he'd do well with a Formula 1 car. You could certainly put him into one with confidence that he wouldn't wreck it. He was intelligent, he always knew the circuit to an inch, he knew the machinery – after all he was an engineer – and he understood what being in good condition is worth..."

That was the final Grand Prix of the season, abbreviated by panic cancellations after the Le Mans disaster in June, and Fangio had won his fourth World Championship with 42 points ahead of Moss (23) and Castellotti (12). It was the last race for the W196 Mercedes but there was still the sports car title to be decided.

A measure of the Mercedes domination in Formula 1 that summer is gained from the detail that went into team preparation and was discussed by Rudi Uhlenhaut with Peter Garnier in *The Autocar* after the W196s had raced for the last time. The team domination mirrored the superiority of Ferrari in new century recent seasons... and for all the same reasons, half a century before.

"The problem is to find, as accurately as possible, the speeds attainable on every part of the circuit, in order to select a ratio that will ensure that the engine is always working within its most efficient speed range – a calculation that has as a basis the engine's power curve, taken in conjunction with the laden weight of the car. Since the weight decreases as the fuel tank is emptied, an average value is taken; the driver's weight is presupposed to be 80kg (176.4lb). By means of wind tunnel tests the car's air resistance figures are known and the rolling resistance, depending on the weight and the speed of the car and the type and pressures of the tyres used, is also taken into consideration.

"Another figure assessed is the increase in tyre diameter caused by centrifugal force, and the coefficient of friction between the tyres and the various types of surface found round the circuit is considered. From this the maximum speeds possible on the various corners and curves are calculated. By means of these figures, too, the braking points can be found; all figures are calculated for both wet and dry conditions.

"Finally, the technicians have at their disposal exact drawings of the circuit with radii at the bends, surface characteristics, widths, variations in altitude, cambers on corners and so on.

"The next step is to draw up a chart showing the tractive effort and, discounting mechanical losses, the acceleration available in each of the five speeds. Tractive effort, higher in the intermediate gears, ranges between some 1,320lb in second – the lowest gear normally used – and 440lb in fifth; the effort available in each gear varies, of course, according to the final ratio used. At Monte Carlo, for example, some 1,100lb were available in third, while at Spa only 660lb were available in the same gear. In establishing the acceleration available several factors are taken into account. When climbing hills, part of the available power is taken up in overcoming gravity and acceleration is reduced; furthermore, even the time spent in gear changing is not overlooked and has been estimated at 0.3sec for each change. Then there are frequently special problems, such as when a ratio adapts itself very well for a circuit except for, say, one short straight where the alternatives are to over-rev or to change gear and lose a certain amount of time. In these cases, drivers are usually advised to stay in the lower gears, as there is always a safety margin; otherwise a higher ratio is fitted.

"A case in point is the tunnel at Monte Carlo where it was calculated that the cars would be travelling at 90 to 100mph as they left the tunnel. But as the exit of the tunnel is not visible from the entrance, it was presumed that drivers would slow slightly which would have made advisable a change in second, third and fourth ratios. (As it turned out, Fangio, in fact, did not slow.) Eventually, times were taken and it was found that the cars were emerging at 96mph which is a very fair correlation of theory and practice.

"At Monza the curves should have been taken at some 155mph but the rough surface cut down the speed and reduced acceleration out of the curves, as drivers had not changed gear at the right speeds."

This discussion between engineer Uhlenhaut and Sports Editor Garnier could have been taking place yesterday with Patrick Head of Williams in conversation with Nigel Roebuck of *Autosport*, with the technician endeavouring to explain what he regarded as the blindingly obvious to the journalist.

The comparison of Garnier in 1955 and Roebuck fifty years later is apposite, since the writers were, and are, regarded as trusted confidantes, members of the inner circle in the Grand Prix paddock. Consider that Garnier was given, for reasons now unclear, a works D50 Lancia Grand Prix car to drive through Monaco traffic on the weekend of the race. And a photograph exists to prove it!

## Chapter 19

# SUNSHINE AND
# SHADOW AT DUNDROD

The Tourist Trophy in Northern Ireland on the seven-mile Dundrod course on the opposite side of Belfast to the pre-war Ards TT circuit, was judged a superb test of road-holding for sports cars but made dangerous with the high banks lining either side of the road for much of the lap. It was, after all, an Irish country road, rather than a race track and compromise was necessary. That compromise couldn't be guaranteed.

The Sports Car Championship had a lot left in it with Ferrari leading on 18 points, Jaguar second on 16, Maserati third on 11 and Mercedes a distant fourth with eight. That would change but those figures make the point that while Mercedes appeared and were dominant, they were not featuring thus far on the championship points standing.

It was the Golden Jubilee year of the TT; 50 years since John Napier had won the first race that carried the Tourist Trophy title, in an Arrol-Johnston from Percy Northey in a Rolls-Royce, averaging 33mph (53.1kph) for the 208-mile (335km) race then held on the Isle of Man. S.C.H. Davis wrote in *The Autocar* a quarter century after that first race:

"The winning car had a two-cylinder engine with the cylinders horizontal and open at each end, the two pistons sliding in each cylinder, the compression space being in the middle. Each piston had a short connecting rod, a rocking lever and a long connecting rod to drive what looked like an ordinary 4-cylinder crankshaft carried immediately below the cylinders, the whole thing being lubricated mainly by hope but theoretically by splash ..."

Richard Hough wrote in his book *Tourist Trophy*, the definitive history of the race, that of the 98 drivers entered for the 84-lap 623-mile (1,002km) TT in 1955 "Perhaps a dozen could be placed in the top class, another two dozen described as very good, the balance ranging from the experienced to the inexperienced. To contemplate 49 cars, with top speeds varying from 100 to 150mph, on the straight after the pits, on a narrow, winding circuit for seven hours – in a year that had been dogged by disaster – was less than reassuring ..."

Mercedes-Benz was determinedly chasing the championship and had three cars for Fangio/Kling, Moss/Fitch, and von Trips/Simon. Jaguar entered one works D-type for Mike Hawthorn and local driver Desmond Titterington.

The inclusion of the 27-year-old German nobleman, Wolfgang von Trips in the Mercedes team, was his first front-line recognition within German motorsport and he was given one of the two special 300SLR 'Carrera' coupés to drive from Germany to Belfast, to acquaint himself with the powerful sports car he would be racing. The coupé was used for Fangio to squire the likes of von Trips around the circuit and show him the lines ... until Jaguar team manager, Lofty England, protested to the race management.

There were three 3-litre Ferraris for Castellotti/ Taruffi, Trintignant/Maglioli and a yellow Ecurie National Belge car for Claes/Swaters. Maserati entered two cars for Behra/Bordoni, and Musso/Musy. Three Aston Martins were entered for Collins/Brooks, Parnell/Salvadori, and Walker/Poore. Among the other ranks, John Dalton was sharing an Austin-Healey with Lance Macklin, Carroll Shelby and Masten Gregory were an all-American pairing in a Porsche, Ron Flockhart and Johnny Lockett were in an MG, Bill Smith was sharing a Connaught with John Young, Mike Anthony and Peter Jopp were sharing a 1,467cc Lotus-MG, Colin Chapman and Cliff Allison were in a 1,097cc Lotus-Climax and Jim Mayers was sharing a Cooper with Jack Brabham.

The draw for the start among the individual cars saw John Young and Bill Smith toss for who would start in the Connaught. The 20-year-old Smith won. And lost. He was a talented young Scot and had won the Ulster Trophy on this same course earlier in the year, so he knew the constraints of the country road course but could not cope with the hand fate dealt him. Jim Mayers decided to start in the Cooper he shared with Jack Brabham and the course of history was changed in that decision. Mayers, 31, son of a wealthy glass manufacturer, and founder of the 'Monkey Stable' of MGs, had also drawn the short straw and took the start.

At the end of the first lap, from the Le Mans start at 10.30am, Moss was leading in the Mercedes from Hawthorn (Jaguar) and Bob Berry who had led away from the start in a D-type Jaguar but was out on the second lap with a puncture. Before the end of the second lap there was an ominous pall of smoke rising into the air in the general direction of Deer's Leap.

*The Autocar* reported: "First news to come through was sparse ... 'There has been an accident at Cochranstown ... three cars involved ... two cars are burning,' and it was some time before these early reports were amplified. It seemed that the pale blue 300SL Mercedes-Benz driven by the Vicomte de Barry had been leading a string of cars down the undulating hill towards Cochranstown. J.C.C. Mayers, possibly trying to overtake the Mercedes, struck a concrete gate-post at high speed. The car caught fire and threw burning fuel on the road. The following drivers found themselves confronted with a wall of flame, and six further cars were involved to a greater or lesser extent."

Peter Jopp described the scene to Peter Miller who recorded it in his book *The Fast Ones*. Jopp had been chatting to Smith while they waited across the road for the Le Mans start, their Lotus and Connaught side by side after qualifying. "We ran for the cars with mine away first and leading him for the first lap. We were then in the second group, lying about 15th and 16th and being badly baulked by the Vicomte de Barry's Mercedes saloon [sic], which was making overtaking difficult by holding the centre of the road.

"During the second lap the Connaught passed my Lotus on acceleration on the hill following Leathemstown Bridge, pulling over to my left and no more than two yards ahead as we swept into the dip before Deer's Leap. Ivor Bueb, just ahead of us in a works Cooper, managed to get through on the left by putting two wheels on to the grass but Jim Mayers, who was trying hard to prove that his privately prepared Cooper was as fast as the works car, found the de Barry Mercedes directly in front of him, going downhill. Jim swerved from left to right, trying to overtake, lost control and mounted the bank, so hitting a concrete gate-pillar.

"The wreckage of the car fell back into the centre of the track bursting into flames, and as Smith and I went over the Deer's Leap together, with all four wheels off the ground, the road directly ahead was blocked by flaming wreckage.

"Ken Wharton's Frazer Nash was ahead of me and pulled over to the right, trying to find a way through. He failed, hit the bank, bounced off and spun across the track to the left-hand bank, where the car caught fire and threw him out on to the track although it did not actually overturn.

"Bill Smith tried to pass on the left, but couldn't avoid the blazing wreckage of Mayer's car. The Connaught hit the bank, digging in and throwing him out. While braking hard, my only hope seemed to be to scrape through on the right. But a photographer scrambling back up the bank got in my way and it was impossible to avoid hitting him before spinning across the road to a stop a few yards behind Ken Wharton's Frazer Nash which was also well alight by this time. Fuel poured across the track so, jumping clear, I ran back to help the marshals who were lifting Bill across the bank and into a field. It seemed he hadn't much chance as he was badly cut about the face. The engine from Mayer's car was still in the road, so I dragged it out of the way, realising that my only injuries were painful burns to one hand and wrist on the skin that had not been covered by overalls or gloves.

"The disc brakes had saved my Lotus from hitting the burning wreckage of Wharton's car, but with his tank likely to explode and the possibility of the experimental magnesium-bodied Lotus catching fire, with even more disastrous results, some marshals helped push it to one side. Bearded Kretschmann, in a works Porsche, drove through the flames into the bank, while Lance Macklin's Austin-Healey also crashed into the bank in avoiding Smith's wrecked Connaught.

"Macklin, sickened by the similarity to the recent Le Mans crash, turned his back on the accident and walked away up the hill with his crash helmet under his arm, and has not raced since ...

"Jim Russell, the last person directly involved, had a fantastic avoidance, missing us all by bouncing the Cooper from bank to bank, badly damaging the car, but avoiding personal injury. Although Wharton was already in the ambulance by then, the marshals seemed to think he was still in the car, but it was, in fact, Jim Mayer's body which had been collected underneath Wharton's car and remained there as the Frazer Nash burned out.

"Wreckage was spread over 150 yards of the track and it was a couple of laps before officials and reserve drivers had arrived via the minor roads leading from the pits. I remember seeing Jack Brabham drive up with several others. I spoke to Stirling's father, Alfred Moss, who asked me what it was like and, while commiserating with me, interrupted, clocked the stopwatch and said, 'There goes the boy!' as Stirling drove by in the Mercedes.

"The only light relief in the terrible accident was the Irish farmer who gave me a lift to the pits in his old car, who said, 'Do you need a priest?' and I said, 'No, I need a drink.' He replied: 'Pity! I always like a priest at a time like this..!'"

Different days. The modern enthusiast, sanitised by safety regulation, has difficulty trying to encompass a comprehensive racing crash like that with fatalities on an Irish country road, with the matter-of-fact, life-goes-on comment of Stirling's father and the farmer who would have preferred a priest.

Stirling, meanwhile was leading and setting new lap records in the Mercedes with Hawthorn in the D-type disputing second place with Fangio. Behind was von Trips on his debut drive in the Mercedes and Collins in the Aston Martin. On the 25th lap Hawthorn pitted for tyres and fuel and Desmond Titterington took over the Jaguar. Moss was flying well clear of the field and yet to stop but the decision was taken for him when his right rear tyre threw a tread and he slammed the bank at Wheeler's Corner. The Mercedes mechanics hacked the battered bodywork away and American John Fitch took over, now in second place with local driver Titterington leading in the Jaguar and putting an easy 10sec a lap on Fitch who could not have been happy on a circuit like nothing he had ever raced on at home. Collins in the Aston had overtaken von Trips for third place but the advantage was lost when Tony Brooks took over and the Aston Martin started misfiring.

Neubauer called Fitch in on lap 36 and an impatient Moss blasted back into the race with the battered 300SLR as rain was starting and after 56 laps he had clawed back Fitch's lost time and re-taken the lead from Titterington's Jaguar.

The Stewards had decided that the Vicomte Hardy de Barry should be black flagged for his baulking role in the second-lap accident and he was charged with alleged unsafe driving. The next day in the newspapers he denied he had been responsible for the crashes, producing a letter from Stirling Moss … and 'other famous drivers'. "It is a lie to say I was blocking the road. I left the road clear. I was at least 150 yards in front of Jim Mayer's car when it crashed. It is impossible for me to have blocked the road for him. When I heard allegations that I may have caused the crash I was furious."

Yellow flags were out at Tornagrough corner on the back stretch of the circuit. Peter Miller: "Richard Mainwaring in an Elva had crashed, the car had overturned and skidded down the track with its driver pinned underneath. It hit the bank and burst into flames with such ferocity that marshals were unable to get near it. Three drivers were dead before the race was halfway through …"

More mayhem was to come when fiery Frenchman, Jean Behra clouted the bank on the infamous Leathemstown section and his Maserati was upside down. This was the crash which cost Behra his ear and he would thereafter wear a plastic ear fitted by a London specialist.

Moss was still disputing the lead with the Hawthorn/Titterington D-type during final pit-stops and Hawthorn was back in for the closing laps. It was raining hard now, the track was slippery and Hawthorn tipped the D-type into a ditch on one lap but recovered. Colin Chapman had been in 14th overall and leading the 2-litre class as well as the Index of Performance but a long pit-stop with a broken oil-pipe late in the race dropped him down the field.

Hawthorn was keeping Moss honest in the final laps but the Jaguar engine blew with two laps to go and the final order was a Mercedes 1–2–3: Moss/Fitch, Fangio/Kling and von Trips/Simon.

It was Moss's 26th birthday and his mother cut him a slice of cake on the tail of the 300SLR after the race. There was a Mercedes star on the icing.

Miller would visit Behra in hospital after the race. "The whole of Jean's face was swathed in bandages and only his blackened eyes and mouth showed through the narrow slits. He hadn't yet been told that his left ear had been completely severed. One elbow and several fingers were broken and heavily splinted. From throat to groin his skin was burnt an angry mauve by his violent impact with the abrasive track and flakes of red paint were still stuck in the wounds. And yet he raised one hand in feeble salute ..."

*Chapter 20*

# JAMES DEAN:
# "TOO FAST TO LIVE,
# TOO YOUNG TO DIE"

James Dean seemed to do things in threes. He gained fame as a movie star and yet he made only three major movies. He loved to race and yet he took part in only three races. He was killed in a road crash on the last day in September 1955 when a student driver with the unlikely name of Donald Turnupseed over-ran a stop sign in Cholame, California, and Dean's new RS1500 Porsche hit him. The James Dean legend started in that instant of impact. The brooding teenager image in leather jacket and jeans came from Dean's performance in the film *Rebel without a Cause*. His other blockbusters had been *East of Eden* and *Giant* which launched after Dean's death and earned him the uncertain honour of being the first actor to receive an Academy Award nomination posthumously for his role in *East of Eden* and the only actor to receive more than one posthumous Oscar nomination.

Acting was work for the 24-year-old actor known as James on stage, but Jim or Jimmy by his mates at the sports car races. He went racing to relax. His first flirtation with speed came on two wheels with a Harley Davidson.

In his Fairmount high school case study in 1948, he wrote "My hobby, or what I do in my spare time, is motorcycle. I know a lot about them mechanically and I love to ride. I have been in a few races and have done well." He was just 17.

Dean didn't really conform to film star standards of behaviour. His romances with starlets were invented by the PR department at Warner Brothers. His idea of getting down and dirty was to work on the engine of his Porsche. He only had two. The first was a 1500 Speedster. His first race was at Palm Springs in March 1955, a six-lapper for production sports cars 1,300–1,500cc with a mix of Porsches and MG TFs. Dean won. The next day he ran in the 27-lap race for sports cars under 1,500cc and he ended up third overall and first in class. As far as the eager young Dean was concerned he had won again. Being beaten by such as Ken Miles and Cy Yedor in their MG Specials was simply an accolade. Next time out at Minter Field near Bakersfield in Southern California at the end of April and it was harder. The field for the SCCA meet (Sports Car Club of America) was stronger but he was still third overall in the under 1,500cc production class. The next day in the open under-1,500cc class he was ninth overall and second in class.

He entered the Speedster at races in Santa Barbara in May and again in September, but never showed. It seemed that the movie moguls were worried that their young superstar could ruin their shooting schedules if he were to crash his Porsche in a weekend race.

Running in the standard classes was losing its appeal for the eager racer whose starring movie roles meant he could afford a competitive ride. The answer was a new

Porsche Spyder 550RS from Johnny von Neumann's dealership where he had met and befriended a young German who had started working in the Porsche factory in 1950 and then moved to California in March, 1955. Rolf Wuetherich was 28 and had worked on the factory racers at Le Mans, Rheims, Avus and the Mille Miglia in 1953 and 1954. It was Wuetherich who suggested that Dean would be an ideal client for one of the new competition cars that had been built in a run of only 90. The 1,500cc four-cylinder engine gave 110bhp at 6,200rpm. It cost Dean $25,000. He nicknamed his new car 'The Little Bastard'.

This new model had performed well in the 1,000-mile Mille Miglia in Italy that summer, winning the class and finishing 8th overall. In the 24-hour race at Le Mans a Spyder 550 won the Index of Performance. Six cars were entered and five finished.

You could imagine that Wuetherich and Dean would hit it off, the German, newly in California and pleased to be a friend of the film star. Dean would have been delighted to meet a young guy with so much racing background and Porsche expertise. His racing mates in the pits didn't see Dean as a film star, just a young guy getting to be good in a Porsche.

James Byron Dean was born on February 8, 1931, in Marion, Indiana. His father was a dental technician and he moved the family to Los Angeles when Jimmy was five. When his mother died, the lad was sent back to be raised by his aunt and uncle on their Indiana farm. After graduating from high school, he moved back to California where he attended Santa Monica Junior College and UCLA. He began acting with James Whitmore's acting workshop and was soon appearing in television commercials and minor roles in films and in stage plays. Whitmore advised him to go to New York for more experience. He soon qualified as a member of the prestigious Actors Studio and was rising in the ranks of TV dramas and a Broadway role in *The Immoralist* in 1954 which earned him a screen test at Warner Brothers for the part of Cal Trask in the movie version of John Steinbeck's novel *East of Eden*. He celebrated his success in this movie by buying his first Porsche. James Dean had one of the most spectacularly brief careers of any screen star, in just one year and in only three movies.

Every star had to start somewhere. It was said that, while a student at UCLA he had three lines in his first small movie and one line in his second.

While Dean was working out his star roles in his Hollywood epics in 1955, Warner Brothers bosses forbade him to race. It was not because he would have been distracted; they wanted to avoid the chance of an accident that could delay shooting ... or worse.

When *Giant* had been completed, Dean was eager to go racing with his new car. Not everyone shared his enthusiasm. When he showed the Porsche racer to thespians Alec Guinness and Grace Kelly he bragged that it would do 150mph. Guinness apparently told him that he thought it looked dangerous; that if he drove it he would be dead within a week. Six days later he was proved right.

He had entered for a race at Salinas and he and Rolf would drive there with the Porsche on a trailer behind their Chevrolet station wagon. Plans changed when they realised that the new car had not been fully run-in. So Dean and Wuetherich would drive the race car and two of

Jimmy's friends would follow in the Chevvy wagon, driven by von Neumann's PR man, Carl von Delius. Carl – Charlie as he was known in California – was the brother of Ernst von Delius who had been killed in an Auto Union in the 1937 German Grand Prix on the Nürburgring. He had been duelling with Dick Seaman's Mercedes when the Auto Union leapt a hump-backed bridge on the long finishing straight and landed askew, taking Seaman's car with it. The Auto Union careered through a wire fence, went end-over-end twice and finished up outside the circuit on the Coblenz road. He died of his injuries the following morning.

There was a lot of fate about that morning.

Charlie took a photo of the pair in the Porsche on Jimmy's camera before they set off. Jimmy was holding Rolf's hand aloft, shouting "Hi! We're going to win!" Rolf was in the right-hand passenger's seat as they set off on a baking Californian morning, aiming to be at Salinas between 9 and 10 o'clock in the evening. After three hours they pulled over at a gas station and refreshment hut at Blackwell Corner in the desert for a cold drink and there met up with Lance Reventlow, son of Woolworth heiress Barbara Hutton, who was having one of his first races at Salinas in a new 300SL Mercedes. In later years he would build and race his Scarab cars in sports car races and, briefly, in Formula 1. Dean and Reventlow arranged to have supper that evening in Salinas. It was an appointment that wouldn't be kept.

Dean had a Coke, Rolf ate an apple and remembered saying to Jimmy "Now don't you run wild in this race. There's a big difference between a 1,500 Super and a Spyder. Feel your way first." The guys in the Chevvy had caught up, and one told Dean to take it easy; that his movie career was going to be more important to him than his car racing. Dean grinned and said he'd be a good boy. Then he did a strange thing. He pulled a ring off his finger and slipped it on to the ring finger of Rolf's left hand, saying "Look Rolf, you are my guardian angel. I'll give you this ring."

In a feature in *Christophorus*, the Porsche house magazine published a few years later, Wuetherich told his story of the accident for the first time. With his smashed mouth he had been unable to speak in the days after the crash and when he could his lawyer suggested that he say nothing, because the inquiry into the responsibility for the accident was still in progress. His then wife was more vocal and although she had not been in any way involved she gave lurid descriptions of the crash. In 1957 a German magazine splashed a feature *"My Death Drive with James Dean"* but Wuetherich had not written it, and in fact knew nothing about it until it appeared in print.

"Jimmy wasn't driving especially fast. The engine still had to be run-in. The speedometer wavered between 60–100mph all the time, sometimes he drove in third gear, sometimes in fourth, mostly between 4,000–6,500rpm. Sitting beside Jimmy, I always had a very safe feeling on the road. I could have slept beside him."

Much has been made of Dean getting a speeding ticket on this trip. At Bakersfield there was a by-pass road with a speed limit of 45mph. Dean usually obeyed these city speed limits but the Porsche racing exhaust caught the attention of a patrol car and he was booked at 50mph. He was fined five dollars for being five mph over the limit.

"The patrolman was very polite and afterwards began to talk to James about the strange car, which very much interested him," Rolf recalled. "They parted on friendly terms."

One of many versions of this incident that appeared in papers after the accident was that the cop had warned Dean that if he drove with such disregard for speed limits he wouldn't live the day out.

It was 5.45pm when they approached a junction where turning traffic had to stop and give way. They were going straight through. The sun was already very low in the sky and shone in their faces. The road went down in a slight depression and up the other side but remained straight.

A 1938 Ford V8 driven by a California Polytechnic student, Donald Turnupseed, was approaching the 'Stop' sign to turn left on to the main road. In those days in that part of the world a Stop sign meant that you slowed down and if nothing was coming you motored on through. Turnupseed was the same age as the man he was about to kill. "I did not see the Spyder," he said later. "I only saw it when it was too late."

The setting sun was throwing reflections on the road and the Porsche was silver, sleek and low. It would have been easy to miss if you were sitting high in a big old Ford. Dean didn't brake. He obviously thought the other driver would stop at the intersection sign. The tyre marks of the Ford showed that Turnupseed had braked hard for 30 metres.

There was a head-on collision between the left side of the nose of the Spyder and the right half of the Ford radiator and bumper. It was estimated that the Spyder was travelling between 80–95mph. Wuetherich was thrown in a high arc out of the car, clear across the intersection and into a field. Dean's camera flew out and was only found a week later. James Dean remained wedged in the car. He had been killed instantly. His neck was broken and the crushed steering wheel had been driven into his body. He suffered major head injuries. The student in the big Ford was practically unscathed.

Wuetherich regained consciousness in the ambulance and he realised that James was strapped to a stretcher below him. It was several days before he was told that Dean had been killed instantly.

Rolf's face had been smashed and his left foot was twisted in a serious and very complicated bone injury that threatened amputation. His mouth was full of jawbone splinters and broken teeth. A few days later Johnny von Neumann insisted that he be transferred to a specialist clinic in Los Angeles, where, by coincidence, Dr Neufeld, a German specialist in bone injuries such as Rolf had suffered, was able to save his leg.

It seemed that the fatal crash was simply a continuation of the James Dean legend. The wreck of the Spyder was bought for $2,500 by car customiser, George Barris. When the wreckage arrived at his garage, the Porsche slipped and fell on one of the mechanics unloading it. The accident broke both his legs. The wreck was broken up and bits sold to other Porsche racers, Troy McHenry and William Eschrid who installed these parts in their own cars. In a race at Pomona Fairgrounds in October 1956, McHenry died when his car, in which the engine from 'The Little Bastard' had been installed, went out of control and hit a tree. Eschrid's car flipped when it suddenly locked up in a corner and he survived serious injuries. A lad, trying to steal the wrecked Porsche's steering wheel, slipped and ripped his arm open on a jagged piece of metal. Another ghoulish souvenir hunter was injured trying to steal a blood-stained piece of upholstery. Barris sold two of Dean's tyres to a customer and within a week, he was involved in a crash when both the tyres blew out simultaneously.

Barris then loaned the wrecked remains of 'The Little Bastard' to the Californian Highway Patrol for a touring display to illustrate the importance of automobile safety. Within days, the garage housing the Spyder was burned to the ground. With the amazing exception of 'The Little Bastard' every other vehicle in the garage was totally destroyed. When the car was put on exhibition at a Sacramento high school, it fell from its display and broke a teenager's hip. It got worse. When car customiser George Barris was hauling the remains of the Spyder on a flatbed truck, he was involved in an accident and was thrown from the cab. The Porsche fell on him and he was killed instantly. The mishaps surrounding 'The Little Bastard' continued until 1960 when it was loaned out for a safety exhibit in Miami, Florida. When the exhibition was over, the wreckage mysteriously vanished en route to Los Angeles by truck and was never seen again.

Donald Turnupseed died of cancer in 1995. It was noted at the time "Turnupseed couldn't swerve out of the way of Dean's Porsche Spyder, but he successfully swerved journalists who frequently pestered him for interviews about the accident."

The James Dean legend lived on. In 1995 *Empire* magazine listed him at No. 42 in their list of "The 100 Sexiest Stars in Film History". Two years later the same magazine had him at No. 33 in the magazine's "The Top 100 Movie Stars of All Time."

One of his co-stars, Natalie Wood said "All of us were touched by Jimmy, but he was touched by greatness." Humphrey Bogart observed "It's a good thing Dean died when he did. If he'd lived, he would never have been able to live up to the publicity." The Eagles penned a lyric about him that went: "Too fast to live, too young to die."

James Byron Dean was quoted as saying: "Dream as if you'll live forever. Live as if you'll die today ..."

*Chapter 21*

# FIRST GRAND PRIX FOR COOPER IN "THE CAR THAT JACK BUILT"

They wouldn't have been aware in October 1955 at Port Wakefield, South Australia that motor racing history was being made and that John Arthur Brabham and Cooper were putting their stamp on it. Jack Brabham, the dark-jowled bloke from the Sydney speedway had come home from the Old Country with a car he had knocked together himself in a corner of the Cooper Car Company in Surbiton, Surrey. It was not a normal Cooper even as Cooper cars were recognised in those days, recently evolving from the ubiquitous mid-engined 500s to front-engined Cooper-Bristols and bob-tailed sports cars with the first 1,100cc Coventry-Climax engines.

Brabham had his own recipe, recognising the potential of the little sports-racer, as the basis for a stretched streamlined single-seater. The stretching was required to accommodate the 6-cylinder 2-litre Bristol engine, originally 'liberated' from the BMW company as part of post-war reparations. The result was not a lovely car to look at, being wrong at all the angles where the 1,100cc bobtails were right, but aesthetics didn't bother Brabham. Always supposing he could have spelled the word – or pronounced it.

225

John Cooper would say "Jack didn't start working *for* the team, as much as working *with* us ..." The car was stretched by two inches in the wheelbase, the chassis tubing was up-rated with larger wheels and brakes, and a central seat was fitted inside the Kamm-tailed fully-enveloping aluminium body fabricated to suit the chassis. Bottom gear was removed from the Citroën/Cooper/ERSA gearbox because the car was so light that first gear wasn't necessary, and also first gear in that gearbox was notoriously weak. The independent front suspension followed traditional Cooper practice with a high-mounted transverse leaf spring and lower tubular wishbones.

The 2-litre Bristol engine (actually 1,971cc) was to have been increased to 2.2-litres to qualify for a Formula 1 entry but although this increase in engine size never happened, the car had apparently been fiddled through for the Grand Prix at Aintree. The engine was said to be a spare from the Bristol team at Le Mans in 1955 and this is easy to believe because Jack was signed as a reserve driver for the Bristol team in the 24-hour race. The 'Brabham Cooper' took just six weeks to build from Jack's original idea to the first blast up the road. The clutch failed on the morning of the Grand Prix at Aintree so Jack had to battle on clutchless until the engine overheated and he retired.

In the team history *Cooper Cars* Doug Nye wrote "Nobody could be blamed for failing to read the writing on the wall ..."

Next time out at Snetterton Jack enjoyed a long dice side by side and nose to tail disputing third place with Moss in his 250F, behind a brace of Vanwalls. Jack spun off in the closing laps and came home fourth, saying then that this was the race that prompted him to keep on racing. "If it hadn't been for that race, I might have gone back to Australia for good."

Jack also raced the car at Brands Hatch, Charterhall in Scotland and Crystal Palace before shipping it home for the summer season in Australia.

In fact there were two of these 'Brabham Coopers' built, with a second car built-up as a two-seat sports-racer for Bob Chase's team by Chase's mechanic, Peter Morris. This car was entered for Mike Keen to drive in the Nine Hour race at Goodwood but he went off the track at Fordwater, the car was launched over corn stooks and it somersaulted several times. The fuel tanks ruptured, the car caught fire and Keen was killed. The car was totally destroyed.

In Australia, Jack entered for a race at Bathurst on October 1st but ran the bearings in practice and never made the grid. Two days later in a busy schedule at Orange, an oil line blew in a preliminary heat and Jack coasted home in second place but the engine was damaged and he was a retirement after one lap in the final. A week later he was at Port Wakefield for the 20th Australian Grand Prix.

The circuit was only 1.3 miles to the lap and there were to be three heats before the 80-lap, 104-mile Grand Prix final the following day. Brabham was third in his qualifying heat behind Reg Hunt in a 250F Maserati and Stan Jones (father of Alan, World Champion in 1980) in the Maybach Special that had been built-up based on an engine from a war-surplus German scout car. Jones had driven this car to win the New Zealand Grand Prix the previous year.

In the Grand Prix, Hunt and Jones were on the front row by virtue of fastest heat times, and Brabham was on the second row beside Tom Hawkes in the Cooper-Bristol recently bought from Jack!

Hunt led away with Jones being harried by Brabham in the opening laps from Hawkes and Neal's Cooper-Bristol. Brabham eventually passed Jones, not having the time to consider the motor racing family dynasty both men would be fathering in Australia. After 25 laps Jack was inside Hunt's leading 250F and that would be the pattern of the race. Jones was having clutch trouble and after a pit stop to check, he was unable to re-start. Doug Whiteford had been coming up through the field in his majestic Lago Talbot having made a tardy start. Lap 68 and he was past Hawkes's Cooper-Bristol into third place but Hawkes was starting to suffer a fuel feed problem that would eventually stop him on the back straight with only two laps to go, and the final result was Brabham (Cooper-Bristol), Hunt (250F Maserati), Whiteford (Lago Talbot), Neal (Cooper-Bristol) and Trenberth (Cooper-Vincent 1000cc).

It was by no means an event counting towards the World Championship but it was a national Grand Prix and as such, a history-maker as Jack Brabham made two marks – he had won the first Grand Prix in a Cooper-Bristol ... and the first Grand Prix in a Brabham-built Grand Prix car!

*Rising Star Takes Grand Prix* ran the headline in the December 1955 issue of the Australian magazine *Wheels*. "Young ex-speedway driver Jack Brabham won his first Grand Prix at Port Wakefield, South Australia, on October 10. Only 29, he is recognised as one of the most polished road racing drivers in Australia, rising to prominence in his 2-litre Cooper Bristol. He won the GP with his new

2.2-litre rear-engined Cooper-Bristol in which he raced abroad." I wonder whether Jack had the bigger 2.2 motor by now, or was he perpetuating the Aintree myth and actually still running the 2-litre?

John Arthur Brabham would spend the rest of his career making racing history and be knighted for his efforts. He won the World Championship for Cooper in 1959 and 1960. In 1961 he took the first Grand Prix car to Indianapolis and finished ninth in the famous '500'. In 1962 he left Cooper and set up his own Brabham team in Formula 1 and in 1966 he won the World Championship in a car with his name on the nose and an Australian Repco V8 engine in the tail. New Zealander Denis Hulme drove a Brabham to win the world title in 1967 with Jack second.

Jack's three sons, Geoff, Gary and David would all race and all won national titles in different categories in different countries. "I warned them when they started, not to spend their own money on racing," said Jack. "So they took my advice ... and spent mine!"

## Chapter 22

# FINAL LAURELS
# IN SICILY

The Targa Florio win almost didn't happen and with it, the sports car championship crown for Mercedes. Alfred Neubauer was under the impression that the race had been cancelled in the wake of the Le Mans disaster and so he had to launch a last-minute mass effort to attend. PR Director Artur Keser had been told by veteran journalist and race reporter, Gunther Mölter at the Frankfurt Show that the race was still on and they were immediately on a deadline to get to Sicily in time.

There were 45 mechanics and a dozen engineers on the move from Stuttgart in 15 passenger cars, six lorries and three radio cars heading south. The Mercedes team for the Targa was made up of two Englishmen, an Irishman, an American, an Argentine and a German: Stirling Moss, Peter Collins, Desmond Titterington, John Fitch, Juan Manuel Fangio and Karl Kling – the only German in the driver line-up for the last race in which the Mercedes-Benz works team would participate.

Alfred Neubauer, the legendary large team manager was indulging himself in his memories of his days, younger and more compact, as a racing driver when he drove a little 1,100cc Ferdinand Porsche-designed Austro-Daimler Sascha in the 1922 race, winning his class and finishing 19th overall. In 1923 he joined the Mercedes team and drove a two-litre four-cylinder car to 15th place and third in class in the 1924 Targa Florio.

Stirling Moss was actually on holiday in the South of France when he received the letter of command to race in the Targa Florio. He had asked for Peter Collins to join him in the same 300SLR sports-racer he had used to win the Mille Miglia and the TT at Dundrod. Collins was contracted to Aston Martin that season but neither Aston Martin nor Jaguar were entering the race in Sicily, so David Brown gave his permission for the two British drivers to race together. They had Mercedes saloons and a 300SL to try and memorise the 45-mile (72.4km) mountain circuit for the 13-lap race over 511 miles (822km) and where all the team drivers seemed to suffer some sort of contact with the local scenery.

The race on the Little Madonie circuit in the mountains above Cerda would be the World Sports Car Championship decider. Ferrari went to Sicily leading with 19 points and Mercedes and Jaguar were tied on 16 points each. The D-type Jaguars were most definitely not designed for this course; more the smooth circuits at Le Mans and airfield tracks like Sebring and Silverstone, so the British team abstained. Mercedes had to finish 1–2 to clinch the title and their cause was aided when Piero Taruffi, winner for Ferrari the previous year, clashed with Enzo Ferrari the week before the race and refused to drive. This reduced the Ferrari team to Castellotti/Manzon and Maglioli/Sighinolfi. Maserati fielded a works car for Musso/Villoresi.

The Targa Florio was like no other race. There were no flag marshals because it was felt that the course was so long that it would be impossible to train enough of the locals to be responsible. Pit signals were another major problem. Moss observed that with a lap taking three quarters of an hour, a single signal from the pits would mean it was immediately well out of date, so Mercedes brought down three radio-equipped cars and stationed these in well-equipped service pits at calculated positions around the circuit. Neubauer would take the times at the main pits and this would be radioed on to be shown to the driver only 25-kilometres later. In true Mercedes fashion these service pits in the Sicilian countryside were equipped with petrol, tyres, tools, a lorry workshop and a dozen German mechanics and signallers in white overalls.

The cars started at half-minute intervals and out on the mountain course overlooking the first of the German service pits, veteran *Autocar* reporter W.F. Bradley, watching through binoculars, saw Moss come through in the lead after his first full standing-start lap with a casual wave to the mechanics, having taken nearly two and a half minutes off Castellotti's lap record set the year before! Making it even more impressive was the fact that Moss had never raced in the Targa before. "Further, instead of stern concentration, Moss appeared to be perfectly at ease, for on the short, rising length between two acute bends, which had necessitated full lock and the use of the gears, he had time to respond by a wave of the hand to the plaudits of the little group of spectators."

Into the fourth lap and Moss was missing. Castellotti's Ferrari was leading in this confusing mountain race.

When Moss eventually came storming through the Mercedes was battered and he was in fourth place, five minutes down on the Ferrari.

"On my fourth lap I came round a left-hand corner and used the left gutter because it straightened the road out so much," Moss wrote later in his personal account of the race. "I got some mud on my left tyres and when I tried to go round a right-hand curve which followed it – I suppose at nearly 100mph – the muddy tyres let the back slide away and I hit the bank on the right, climbing half way up it, bounced back onto the road and spun. I then headed for what I thought was a precipice on the left-hand side of the road. Fortunately it was only about a 6ft drop, with a sloping field beyond. The car shot off the road, went down into the field and landed on a great big piece of rock. I couldn't move the car because the wheels were off the ground and it was balanced on the rock, only a couple of inches, perhaps, over its normal height.

"Luckily, although it was well out in the wilds, there were a lot of people watching and 50 or 60 of them came running across the fields. The car seemed pretty bad to me, but our six minutes' lead drove me on to try and get it out. With the help of these people – after most of them had taken some pictures – we managed to get it off the rock. I then drove along the field looking for a place to regain the road because the bank was, I suppose, about 50 degrees inclination and obviously too steep just to drive up. I found a place that was about 45 degrees and took a run at it, but couldn't get up much more than 15mph because of mud from rain the night before, and I got wheel-spin. However, helped by 30 or 40 people, on my twelfth attempt, the car just toppled over the top. I went screaming off but the car felt a bit funny. After about 50 yards I realised I hadn't done my crash hat up, because it blew off. So I stopped, reversed and, picked it up and started off again."

The car was relatively undamaged but the engine had overheated in the off-road antics and a lot of the water had boiled away. Stirling drove 40 kilometres to the main pits where the mechanics changed tyres, refuelled, bashed and hacked at the damaged bodywork and topped up with 10 quarts (11.36 litres) of water. It turned out that the chassis had been slightly bent in Stirling's off-course escapade but nothing could be done about that. Collins took over and set about making up lost time. They were now down in fourth place behind Fangio, Castellotti and Titterington. Peter was soon in the mood for the chase in his first drive for Mercedes.

He was tailing a Ferrari which suddenly braked hard and Peter had to swerve sharply left. "It was a right-hand corner with a big stone embankment on the right and, I think, a sheer drop on the left," Collins wrote later for *Autocar*. "Anyway there was a little parapet there about two feet high. Swinging rather abruptly to the left, I had to oversteer the car a little, and got on to the gravel where, of course, the adhesion went, and although I put my brakes on, I shunted the wall fairly hard. Fortunately it was a very poorly built wall – it seemed to crumble away, and I finished up with the front wheels poking very near the edge.

"I didn't stop to get out and see how far down it was, and as the back wheels still had adhesion, I reversed out and continued, passing the Ferrari that had put me off, further up the road."

He stopped at the Campofelice Mercedes service pit where the mechanics were keen to straighten the damaged front, but the car seemed easily driveable so rather than risk losing further time, Collins stormed off, actually getting back to lead the race before handing over to Moss for the final stint. Stirling observed that the car was now scarcely in showroom condition but he held his lead until the finish just after 5pm, breaking the lap record time after time. He finished nearly five minutes ahead of Fangio/Kling who were the same distance ahead of the Castellotti/Manzon Ferrari. The Titterington/Fitch 300SLR was fourth and Mercedes had won the World Sports Car Championship by just one point.

It was the last time that Stirling was to drive his famous 300SLR officially in anger.

*Chapter 23*

# TONY BROOKS WINS IN SYRACUSE

It was one of those trumpeted and very unlikely race victories that almost never happened and yet when the race in Syracuse was over on October 23, a British driver in a British car had won a foreign Grand Prix – for the first time since Segrave won the San Sebastian Grand Prix for Sunbeam in 1924! The Syracuse GP was won by Tony Brooks in a Connaught.

It was all so last-minute. Connaught had never raced abroad and yet they had chosen the furthest race in the calendar at the very end of the hectic 1955 season. Then there was the problem of drivers. Few were committed to the Syracuse race but it seemed that few wanted, or were able, to go. The week before the race, *The Autocar* addressed the problem on Connaught's behalf, almost whimsically: "Although on paper we have plenty of good drivers, it is surprising how few are really available when they have been whittled down for one reason or another. First come the inevitable questions – has he had any long-distance experience? What is his crash record like? Is he used to handling cars of similar speed and power? Then comes the biggest bugbear of the lot and one that is often referred to and grumbled over – is he under contract with an oil company whose products are not used by the cars concerned? And if so, can he be released in time (if at all) from his contract – or the team for which he is signed to drive?

"Reg Parnell, Connaught's first driver, cannot go to Syracuse because of business commitments over the Motor Show period. Peter Collins? Probably driving for Maserati; if not, they'll have first preference and there is no time to find out and get a release if necessary. Mike Hawthorn? Probably driving for Ferrari... anyway, he's signed up with Shell. Desmond Titterington? Could be driving for Ferrari... quick phone call... no, too many business commitments. Bob Gerard? Can't spare the time from his business. Roy Salvadori? No good; driving the Gilbey Engineering Maserati at Syracuse already. Alan Brown? Ill in bed. Stirling Moss? No, not Moss; signed with Shell (Connaughts use Esso). Les Leston? Tony Brooks? Ivor Bueb as reserve driver? And so on, and on..."

It was interesting that Leston and Brooks were mentioned almost last as prospective drivers, when they were the two finally signed for the race. Neither had driven a Formula 1 car before.

The Connaught team was the fruition of a dream by a pair of ex-RAF pilots, Rodney Clarke and Mike Oliver, who would join forces and set up a company called Continental Cars as a Bugatti dealership after the war. The French company failed to face the post-war market so the pair concentrated on selling used Bugattis instead.

The name Connaught was actually created as a mishmash combination of *Con*-tinental and the word *aut-*

omobile. They built cars for Formula 2 and then Formula 1 in the early 1950s as the Grand Prix grandees came and went and for a few seasons, F2 became F1 to maintain the grids.

Brooks still believes that he was picked to drive for the team in Sicily "because they couldn't find anyone else at short notice." He had never driven the car before and he was racing against the Maserati works team on a track he had never seen before. The 23-year-old had spent the flight to Syracuse studying his dental textbooks for an upcoming examination at the dental hospital in Manchester.

He had started racing in 1952 with a Healey Silverstone and the following summer he was in a Le Mans Replica Frazer Nash. In 1954 he had been signed to drive the works de Dion-axle 'Nash and by 1955 he had been signed by John Wyer to drive for Aston Martin at Le Mans, Goodwood and the Tourist Trophy. He was also racing a privately-entered 2-litre Connaught Formula 2 single-seater and was offered a sports car drive by the Connaught team at Aintree where he finished second to Colin Chapman's Lotus after an exciting duel with Les Leston in the other team Connaught. It was this drive that earned him selection for the Grand Prix in Syracuse at the end of the 1955 season.

There was only a week to spare when the financial arrangements were finally agreed with the race organisers. It is worthwhile exploring the detail of the effort involved in the tiny team embarking on what, in anyone's terms, was a mammoth venture to the other end of Continental Europe.

Mike Oliver, Connaught's engine development expert, was to be team manager. 'Benny' Benstead was chief mechanic in charge of Brooks's car; John Linch looked after the Leston car. Other mechanics were Joe Wilkins, Rod Dore and Dickie Samuelson. Each Connaught had its own 1938 AEC diesel transporter which had started life as Green Line buses and were then converted to carry racing cars and their spares.

Oliver was driving his Ford Zephyr.

The transporters crossed the Channel to Dunkirk on the Saturday night but were stopped at the French port because they did not have the requisite paperwork. The permits had been applied for but not received, so Oliver had to drive to the various French government offices from Le Touquet to Dunkirk, on to Lille and then back to Dunkirk, where the transporters were finally given permission to leave at noon on the Monday.

Practice started on Friday in Syracuse, so for the little Connaught team, the race was starting now and they only had two drivers per transporter. The first stint was from noon Monday until 3am on the Tuesday morning when they stopped for a brief sleep in Chalons. On Tuesday after a 7am start they went over the Mont Senis Pass to Alessandria, arriving at midnight. Another dawn start and they drove in convoy all day and through the next night to Rome and on to Naples, with Mike Oliver driving ahead, arranging meals for his team like pit-stops in a race.

These pensioned-off coaches were popular for racing transporters but they tended to suffer from the constant pace and mountain passes, and the brakes were suffering on the transporter carrying Brooks's Connaught. Having been driven hard for yet another day, by the Thursday night most of the braking was being done on the pre-selector gearbox. When they reached Cosenza the crews decided to stop over in a hotel for much-needed sleep. The next morning Brooks's crew would tend the transporter brakes, and the Leston transporter would make an early start alone.

It left at 7.30am. The others had to improvise, compensating somehow for lining wear by means other than re-lining because there were no available parts and less time. They built up the brake cams with packing, an operation carried out with the help of a local on a Vespa who ferried them to and from a nearby garage. They only managed to do the back brakes and by 10am they were on the road again. In an age before mobile phones, Brooks and Leston would have been unaware of the endless problems being undergone by their long-suffering mechanics.

When they reached the ferry at the Italian mainland town of Villa San Giovanni on the Friday evening they found that the first ferry would not take commercial vehicles, so they were forced to wait for the next ferry in a queue of family Fiats, but somehow they made sure of forcing their way on board. They made it to Messina but the exhausted crew still faced 110 miles (177 kilometres) of mountain roads to Syracuse. It looked as though they would at least make it for Brooks to drive on the final day of practice ... but in Catania the engine of the transporter cut dead. Joe Wilkins tracked the problem to a loose plug in the fuel filter, and they finally reached Syracuse at 3am on the Saturday morning, seven hours after the transporter carrying Leston's car and five days after leaving England.

Brooks and Leston had hired Vespa motor scooters to learn the circuit and this was all the track knowledge they had. Leston was in the Connaught streamliner, and Brooks was in the open-wheeled car. The opposition included five works Maseratis for Musso, Villoresi, Schell, Luigi Piotti and Carroll Shelby, two works Gordinis for Manzon and Pollet, four private Maseratis for Horace Gould, Salvadori, Valentario, and Rosier and two private Ferraris.

The B-Series Connaught had been built to take the 2.5-litre V8 'Godiva' engine from Coventry-Climax but when this failed to appear, Connaught reverted to the 240bhp four-cylinder Alta engine. As set up for that end-of-season race in Syracuse, Brooks's Connaught was fitted with fuel injection and disc brakes.

Leston had a bad cold and his car developed an air lock early in the session, so that he had little chance for practice. Brooks found his way around gently for a few laps. His driving technique was unflurried and the Maserati drivers were content to relax in the pits and rely on their times set the previous day … until the public address announced that Brooks had just set fastest lap of the session!

Suddenly the Maseratis were being warmed up and their drivers were out on the course. Musso's best was pole at 2min 3.8sec and Villoresi had turned 2min 4.2sec.

To the amazement of everyone, Brooks, who had never seen the circuit other than from the saddle of his hired scooter, had qualified on the outside of the front row beside two works Maseratis.

He had not had the time to practice a start with the 2.5-litre car and was anxious not to break the 'box with too much enthusiasm off the line. Oliver had asked his two drivers to stay with the leaders but not be tempted into any unnecessary action in the early stages. On the first lap Musso led from Villoresi, Schell, Brooks and Leston. Salvadori was 11th and Gould 12th. On the third lap Leston spun and dropped to 12th but Brooks passed Schell and Salvadori had a narrow escape passing a Gordini. He hit the wall in taking avoiding action, buckled a front wheel and stopped at the pits for a replacement.

On lap eight Tony was up to second place. "They told me not to rev over 7,000rpm so I thought it would be wiser to stay under 6,500rpm." Over the next seven laps Brooks overhauled Musso in the lead and on lap 15 he was ahead, saving his novelty new disc brakes and letting Musso pass him into the hairpin only to pass him on the way out. "Without realising it, he was playing cat-and-mouse with Musso and he had completely demoralised the Italian," wrote Denis Jenkinson in his *Motor Sport* report. Doing Musso's head in, would have been a modern description.

A contemporary report suggested that Brooks's tactics were largely dictated by the behaviour of his Connaught and Musso's Maserati at the hairpin. "At the time when it seemed they were scrapping for the lead, Brooks was usually in front on the approach to the hairpin. His acceleration out of it was much superior to the Maserati which is accounted for by the fact that the Connaught-developed four-cylinder Alta engine had better torque at low and medium speeds than the six-cylinder Italian engine; an advantage which even a five-speed gearbox could not overcome."

Put yourself in Musso's place, Italian champion and Maserati team leader, being comprehensively beaten by a British driver he had probably never even *heard* of.

"Having established that he could draw away from Musso, he did so with no great effort after lap 22, and then proceeded to lap the rest of the field. In the meantime Gould had pulled up to sixth, Shelby was fourth and Schell fifth. Salvadori was out with a split fuel tank and Leston was making up the ground he had lost with his early spin. On lap 30 Brooks had lapped all but Musso and Villoresi in the works Maseratis and five laps later he had lapped Villoresi. It wasn't a race, it was a *rout!* On lap 39 the order was Brooks, Musso, Villoresi, Gould, Schell, Shelby and after 70 laps (238.7-miles/384.1km) Brooks was a clear winner, 55sec ahead of Musso. He had lapped the rest of the field twice, averaging 99.05mph (159.4kph) with a new lap record at 102.34mph (164.67kph) on the 54th lap. He broke Marimon's record on three occasions, and his best lap was five seconds faster than his qualifying time!

"At a time when the drivers of British cars were only supposed to watch Italian Ferraris and Maseratis disappear into the distance," wrote Alan Henry in *50 Years of World Championship Grand Prix Racing,* "this was a truly memorable change of script ..."

English privateer, Horace Gould finished fourth in his 250F Maserati, while Les Leston had spoiled his chances of a good finish in the streamlined Connaught with his spin.

The Italian organisers, perhaps prompted by the Maserati team management, demanded that the engine in Brooks's Connaught be stripped and checked for size but all was in order. Just getting to the race at all had been challenge enough for the tiny cash-strapped team, never mind any Machiavellian ideas of running a cheater engine...

*Chapter 24*

# EPILOGUE:
# THE 300SLR COUPÉ:
## A RACER THAT NEVER RACED

The 300SLR Coupés were built for the 1955 Carrera PanAmericana but the race was cancelled in the wake of the Le Mans disaster, ironically involving a Mercedes 300SLR which somersaulted into the crowd killing over 80 spectators and the driver, Pierre Levegh.

Mercedes racing engineer Rudi Uhlenhaut used one of those very special Mercedes as his personal transport for a time and revelled in the complaints about the noise. He said the noise problem was easily and inexpensively cured – wear earplugs.

Born and partly brought up in Britain by an English mother and German father, Uhlenhaut was the engineer who had saved the Mercedes Grand Prix programme when he was appointed Technical Director of the racing division in August1936, aged 30. The major problem was that no-one in the racing department could drive racing cars and they had to rely on what the racing drivers told them, in an era when bravery was in more abundance than engineering skill.

Uhlenhaut told author, Chris Nixon "When I started my new job I took two cars to the Nürburgring and began to learn how to drive a racing car, which is not difficult until you want to go fast, which you're going to have to do if you're going to find out what's wrong with it. Gradually I developed my skills until I could lap the 'Ring (and Monza and Hockenheim) almost as fast as our Grand Prix drivers! I loved driving the racing cars, but I never raced so I can't say if I'd have been a good racing driver or not. I had the technique but I also had the track to myself, which made things a lot easier."

Laurence Pomeroy, technical editor of *The Motor* and author of the two-volume epic *The Grand Prix Car* in the 1950s, was awestruck. Gobsmacked, as we would say in the idiom of today. He had noted that the Mercedes sped from 0–100mph (0–161kph) in 12sec, took just 4.5sec to get from 90–110mph (145–177kph) and only 6.5sec between 110 and 130mph (177 and 209kph). Top speed was around 180mph (290kph). "Uhlenhaut told me that the car will average between 13 and 15.5 miles per gallon on cross country journeys, a tribute to the low specific fuel consumption for the engine and the low drag of the car. But it was not speed, acceleration, steering or fuel consumption by themselves that impressed me but a conjunction of virtues which puts motoring on an entirely new plane, and gives to the experienced driver a greater margin of safety than anything before known at potential average speeds higher than any yet enjoyed ..."

Gordon Wilkins was another of only a handful of journalists allowed to road test the 3-litre straight-eight 300SLR GT in 1955 and he wrote "The switch starts the electric fuel pump and a touch on the starter sets the engine going with a stupefying noise composed of the clatter of valves and the fuel injection pump, the whine of gears, and a general indescribable hammer and boom, magnified by the closed coachwork. Earplugs are obligatory; they reduce the noise, but make conversation impossible.

"The Mercedes magnesium alloy body was long, low and elegant and based more on the Formula 1 W196 streamliners than the slightly dumpy (by comparison, it should be hastily added!) racing 300SLs that had won Le Mans and the Carrera in earlier seasons originating from the radiator ducting in the nose section, was very noticeable."

When Wolfgang von Trips joined the Mercedes line-up for the Tourist Trophy race at Dundrod in Northern Ireland in September, 1955, Uhlenhaut suggested that he drive the 300SLR coupé from Stuttgart to Ireland to become accustomed to the power and handling. The car was used as a 'T' car in practice and Fangio took Kling and Trips round for several laps showing them the Irish ropes until Jaguar team management spotted this and put an official stop to it.

Now the pair of original 300SLR coupés is on display in the Mercedes museum in Stuttgart.

Tony Merrick had earned a name as a skilled racer of historic cars and he had established a specialist company that had created new bodywork and fuel tanks for a W154 Grand Prix Mercedes that had sat on display since 1938 as a stripped chassis in the Deutsches Museum in Munich. The quality of his work in literally re-creating the heroic old Grand Prix car had earned an invitation from Mercedes-Benz museum directors to meet with them and discuss a series of important restoration projects. First he restored a 1902 Simplex as a ground-up project. Next was a very special 300SLR coupé built in 1955 and he was invited back to the factory to discuss the work.

Merrick took his wife on the trip. It was agreed that the coupé would be sent for restoration but when it eventually arrived, Mrs Merrick pointed out that the 300SLR coupé was *not* the car Tony had checked out at the museum. How could she possibly know? Surely there could only have been one of these amazing racing coupés? There had been no mention of a twin. Mrs Merrick, with wifely logic, pointed out that the upholstery was different. The car they had seen at the museum had blue trim, while the car sitting in their workshop had red trim. Tony telephoned the museum in Germany, to be greeted by the embarrassed news that, er, ahem, a mistake seemed to have been made, Herr Merrick. The wrong car had been sent. A lorry eventually arrived and took the coupé back ... but did not deliver the other car.

Tony assumed the deal was off, until a few weeks later two trucks arrived carrying *both* coupés for his restoration!

The Uhlenhaut car had been most used and Merrick's men had to treat 700 cracks on the magnesium alloy body. During the restoration, Tony took it upon himself to remove an engine and take it apart for rebuild ... until he reached the cylinder head studs which had *serrated* nuts. "I'd only ever seen nuts like that on an industrial diesel," said Tony. "We didn't have a tool that would cope, so I phoned the factory again and there was another embarrassed pause." How did Herr Merrick know about the serrated stud nuts? Because he was stripping the engine. But he wasn't supposed to be *touching* the engine. They would make immediate arrangements for it to be returned to the factory. Tony pointed out that it might be easier to send the tool to England than send the engine to Germany, so a compromise was reached whereby a Mercedes mechanic was sent over with the tool and instructions to do the rebuild. "He didn't speak English and I couldn't speak German but after a good dinner with a few bottles of wine, we agreed that we could work together on the engine rebuild.

"We actually had a workshop manual for the engine and when we pulled the engine down it needed new pistons, so I noted the part number and phoned Mahle Pistons in Germany. More embarrassment. The special part number was for a very special car, and how had Herr Merrick come by it? Tony explained the factory restoration commission and was amazed to find that Mahle had a spare set of 300SLR pistons in stock!

"Mercedes used desmodromic valves in some of their engines with the last bit of the valve closure done by a hairspring – but *not* on the SLR. It was compression that finally closed the SLR valve. On the bench, you could turn the engine over slowly with one finger; there was no compression because there wasn't sufficient blow to shut the valves. Everything was roller bearing. There was no friction whatever. If you parked it on a hill in gear it would creep down the hill... It really was an amazing engine.

"On the dashboard of the 300SLR sports car there were four buttons alongside each other. Each little pump was connected to each of the brake back-plates to squirt oil on to the brake shoes. If they had a grabbing brake, they squirted oil onto the brake to stop it grabbing. On the coupé that equipment was there but not connected.

"Those cars were such a delight to work on."

Tony recalled working on the first of the racing Mercedes for the Deutsches Museum. "They sent the original full-size blue linen drawings of the bodywork on the W154 and we laid them all out on the lounge floor. There were eight or ten of them that made up the centre line sections, with template shapes at every 100mm station. We had a Grand Prix Mercedes spread out on our carpet!"

# INDEX

Figures in *italics* refer to illustrations

Abecassis, George 48, 53, 130
Acat, 151, 153
Ace Records 103, 110
Adenauer, Dr Konrad 132
AEC transporter 239–240
Agabashian, Fred 98
Agip petrol 49
Aintree circuit 26, 129, 168–170, 174–175, *179–181*, 226, 229, 238
Albert Park circuit 32
Aley, John 43
Alfa Romeo 29, 42, 90–91, 105, 112, 116–117, 121, 123, 199
  P2 82, 116–117
  P3 Tipo B 116
  Tipo 158 91
Allen, James 44
Allen, Nigel 44
Allison, Cliff 208
Alpine Rally 127
Alta engines 19, 241–242
Alvis 25
American Automobile Association 128
Amon, Chris 18, 170
Andrews, Eamon 23
Anthony, Mike 208
Ardmore airfield circuit 27, 31
Ards TT circuit 77, 126, 206
Argentine GP
  1953 92
  1955 33–38, 92, 170
  1956 122
  1958 26
Arrol-Johnston 206

Ascari, Alberto 33–36, 64, *73, 75*, 81–86, 88–93, 96, 116, 118, 129, 140
  fatal crash *74*, 88–93, 111, 120
  Monaco harbour crash *73–74*, 84–85, 87, 89, 103, 120
  pole positions 119
  race wins 91–92, 118
  superstitions 82, 88–90, 117
  World Championship titles 31, *73*, 92
Ascari, Antonio 82, 90–91, 117
Ascari, Tonino 117
Aston Martin 41, 43, 115, 143, 145, 194–196, 208, 212, 231, 238
  DB3S 53
Austin 127
  B-series twin-cam engine 127
Austin-Healey 133–134, 140–141, 147, 172, *181*, 208, 211
  100S 53, *78*, 124, 127–130, *177*
  100/4 32, 124, 127, 130
Australian GP 1955 190, 227–228
Austro-Daimler Sascha 231
Auto Union 29, 116, 169, 176, 219
*Autocar* magazine 12, 47–48, 53–54, 96, 99, 113, 137, 144, 160, 164, 174, 202, 206, 209, 232, 234, 236
Automobile Club de L'Ouest 151, 153

*Autosport* magazine 12, 43, 103, 124, 172, 204
Avus 217

Bamford, Anthony 60–61, *72*
Bamford, J. C. 60
Bandini, Lorenzo *76*, 85
Barcelona 119
Barrichello, Rubens 59
Barris, George 222–223
Bathurst circuit 227
Bayol, Eric 33
Baxter, Raymond 63, 83–84, 108
Behra, Jean 33–35, 64, 82–83, 85, 112, 114, 166, 169, 172, *187*, 194, 201, 208, 213–214
Belgian GP
  1924 116
  1939 114
  1953 92
  1955 77, 111, 120, 170
Benstead, 'Benny' 239
Bentley 139
  Mark VI 24
  Series 'S' 24
  Vanden Plas sports-tourer 28–29
Bentley, John 96–97, 99
Berry, Bob 208
Bertil, Prince *182*, 194
Bettenhausen, Gary *75*
Bettenhausen, Tony 98, 102
Bianchi motorcycles 90
Bira', Prince 'B. 17, 27–32, *65*
Birger, Pablo 33, 35
Blakeley, Dr 40, 42
Blakeley, David 24, 39–44, *67–68*
Bloemaker, Al 99

BMW 225
Bogart, Humphrey 224
Bonneville 128
Bordoni, 208
Bouillon, Mme 135
Boyd, 98–99
Brabham *190*, 229
Brabham Cooper 226–227
Brabham, David 229
Brabham, Gary 229
Brabham, Geoff 229
Brabham, Jack 32, 96, 171, 175–176, *190*, 208, 211, 225–229
Bradley, W. F. 137, 232
Brands Hatch circuit 227
  Kent Cup 43
Brescia Automobile Club 139
Bristol 43, 226
  engines 171, 225–226
British GP
  1948 91, 169
  1949 30
  1951 169
  1954 170
  1955 26, 129, 168–176, *179–181*, 226
  1956 122
British Motor Corporation 26, 124
  Mini Minor 26
British Racing Drivers' Club 11, 28, 171
  badge 41, 46, *71*
  British Empire Trophy 41
  Road Racing Gold Star 28
Brivio, 91
BRM 171
Brooklands circuit 27–28, 41, *65*, 169, 196
  Mountain Handicap 41
Brooks, Tony 11, 21, *76*, 107, *192*, 208, 236–244
Brown, Alan 237
Brown, David 231
Bucci, Clemar 33
Bueb, Ivor 139, 144–145, 209, 237
Buenos Aires circuit *66*, 119
Buenos Aires GP 1949 91
Bugatti 86, 237
  Type 251 26

Campari, 116
Campbell, Donald 24
CanAm 96
Canestrini, Giovanni 45
Caracciola, Rudolf 46, 63–64
Carrera PanAmericana 247
  1953 118
  1954 130
  1955 cancelled *192*, 245

Castagneto, Renzo 45
Castellotti, Eugenio 33, 35, 53, 55, 64, 82, 86, 88–89, 111, 114–115, 119–120, 140–141, 172–173, *191*,194–195, 199–202, 208, 231–232, 234–235
Chakrabongse, Prince Chula 27, 29–30
Chapman, Colin 117, 208, 213, 238
Charterhall circuit 227
Chase, Bob 227
Chevrolet *75*
Chimay circuit 30
  *GP de Frontières* 30
Chiron, Louis 91
*Christophorus*, Porsche house magazine 220
Chrysler 112
Churchill, Sir Winston 24
Cisitalia 91
Citroën 226
  DS19 24
  2CV 46
  11cv 24
Claes, Johnny 139, 208
Clark, Jim 96
Clarke, Rodney 21, 237
Collins, Peter 32, 42, 53, 122, 145, 171, *190–191*, 194, 200, 212, 230–231, 234–235, 237
Connaught 11, 19, 21, 140–141, 144, 173, 175–176, *192*, 193, 208–211, 236–239, 242–243
  B-Series 241
Continental Cars 237
Continental tyres 199
Cook, Humphrey 40–43, *68*
Coombs, John 43
Coon, Frank 96
Cooper, John 162, 226
Cooper 26, *72*, 86, 96, 162, 171, 174, 208–209, 225, 229
  500 225
Cooper-Bristol 32, 175, *190*, 225, 228–229
Cooper-JAP 173
Cooper-Norton 196
Cooper-Vincent 228
Cortese, 91
Cosworth DFV V8 engine 117
Coventry Climax engines 19, 117, 160, 225, 241
Crystal Palace circuit 227
Cunningham 25
Cunningham, Briggs 25, 144

*Daily Telegraph* 168

Daimler 57
Daimler-Benz AG 146, 154, 156–157
  Press conference re Le Mans tragedy 154–159
Dalton, John 208
*Dance with a Stranger* film 40
Darvi, Bella 81
Davis, Cliff 43
Davis, S. C. H. 206
Davison, Lex *65*
de Barry, Vicomte Hardy 209–210, 212
de Portago, Marquis 105
Dean, James 22, *189*, 215–224
  fatal accident 23, *189*, 215
  racing 22, *189*, 215–220
Delahaye 173
Delamont, Dean 172
Desmond, Kevin 82, 89
Deutsches Musuem 247, 250
Dieppe circuit 27
Disneyland, California 23
Donington circuit 169, 196
Dore, Rod 239
Dreyfus, René 173
Duckworth, Keith 117
Dundrod circuit 46, 127, *186*, *189*, 206, 231, 247
Dunlop disc brakes 127, 162
Dutch GP
  1953 92, 129
  1955 164, *178*

Eagles, The 224
Earls Court Motor Show 77, 126
*East of Eden* film 22, *189*, 215, 218
Ecurie Bleue 173
Einstein, Albert 24
Elisian, Ed 101
Elkhart Lake 25
Ellis, Georgie 39–40, 42–43
Ellis, Ruth 24, 39–44, *67*
Elva 213
*Empire* magazine 223
Emporer-HRG 42–43, *68*
Enever, Syd 125
England, Lofty 134, 141, 143, 145, 207
Englebert tyres 122
Equipe National Belge 139, *187*, 208
ERA 17, 27–29, 41, *68*
Eschrid, William 222
Esso 237
Everett, Rupert 40

Fabi, Teo 23
Fairfield, Pat 27

Fangio, Juan-Manuel 18, 22,
26, 33–38, 48, 54, 55, 59,
63, *66, 74, 76, 78–79,*
81–83, 86–87, 92, 96,
107, 115, 134, 138, 140,
143–144, 146–147, 150,
152, 156, 159, 161,
165–166, 168–169,
171–174, *178–182, 185,
187, 191,* 194, 200–202,
204, 207, 211–212, 230,
234–235, 247
comments on Le Mans
tragedy 148
lap records/fastest laps 64,
77, 83, 112, 114
Mille Miglia trial run 51–52
pole positions 64, *75,* 93,
119, 195
race wins 36–37, *66,* 77,
115, 118, 122
World Championship titles
45, 122, 202
Farina, Nino 33, 35–38, 63,
96, 112, 114–115,
199–200
Faroux, Charles 64
Faure, Edgar 132
Ferrari 25, 33–38, 53–55, 62,
64, *65, 72, 74, 76,* 83–85,
92, 96, 107, 113–115,
120–122, 129–130, 132,
140–141, 145, 162, 166,
170, 172–173, 175, *182,
187, 191,* 194–195,
199–200, 202, 206,
231–235, 241
junk yard *72,* 85
sound impersonations 105
team in decline 22, 59
Ferrari models and engines
'Indianapolis' 53
Squalo 22
Super Squalo 555 63,
199–200
Tipo 375 92, 96
Tipo 500 31
Tipo 625 63, *72*
Tipo 815 90
V6 engines 60, 122
V8 engines 60
V12 engines 60, 92
116F, 2.5-litre twin-cylinder
engine 22, 59–62, *71–72,*
121
500 92
750 Monza 25, 88–89
750S 37–38
Ferrari, Dino 122–123
Ferrari, Enzo 61, 63, 90–91,
107, 112, 122–123, 169,
231
Lancia team taken over 121

FIA 158, 194
FIAT/Fiat 116–117, 121
Topolino 47
Findlater, Anthony 42–43
Findlater, Seaton 42
Fisher, Carl 95
Fitch, John 53, 144, 161,
166, *189, 191,* 207, 212,
214, 230, 235
Flockhart, Ron 53, 127, 130,
208
Flynn, Joe 126
Ford
F100 100
Zephyr 239
1938 V8 221–222
Formula 2 30, 92, 129, 238
Formula 3 173
Formule Libre 34, 37
Frankfurt Motor Show 230
Frazer Nash 128, 210–211
Le Mans Replica 238
French GP
1925 82, 90, 117
1948 91
1954 22, 31
1955 cancelled 166
1956 26
Frère, Paul 112–113, 115,
139, 143–144

Ganley, Howden 171
Gardner, Derek 61
Gardner, 'Goldie' 125
Garnier, Peter 144, 174, 202,
204–205
Gaze, Tony 31–32, *65*
*Gazzeta dello Sport* 45
Geier, 146
Gendebien, Olivier 115
Gerard, Bob 237
German GP 168
1937 219
1953 92, 200
1955 cancelled 194
1956 122
*Giant* film 23, *189,* 215, 218
Gilbey Engineering 173,
237
Girling disc brakes 163
Gonzales, Froilan 33–38, 96,
162, 169
Goodwood circuit 84, 196,
238
Nine Hour race 227
Gordini 22, 33, 35, 64, 112,
175, 241–242
Gordini, Amèdée 107
Gould, Horace 32, 241–243
*Grand Prix of Gibraltar, The*
record *76,* 104–110
Gregory, Masten 208
Guinness, Alec 218

Hamilton, Duncan 26, 194
Hamilton, Maurice 49
Harley-Davidson 215
Harry Ferguson Research 26
Hawkes, Tom 228
Hawthorn, Mike 42, *78–79,*
89, 96, 112, 132, 134,
139–141, 144–146,
149–150, 152, 166, *182,
187,* 200, 207–208,
212–214, 237
Hayley, Bill 23
Head, Michael 194–196
Head, Patrick 194, 196, 204
Healey Silverstone 238
Healey, Donald 53, 127–128,
130–131
Healey, Geoffrey 130
Hedemora 196
Helsinki 196
Henry, Alan 49, 243
Herrmann, Hans 33, 36,
48–49, 52, 55, 63–64, 81,
87, 96, 168
Heuss, Prof Theodor 132
Hill, Graham 76
Hill, Phil 25, *76,* 105, 107,
113
Hockenheim 246
Hopkins, Lindsey 96–97
Hough, Richard 207
Hounslow, Alec 77, 126
Howe, Earl 11
Hoyt, Jerry *75,* 98
HRG 42–43
Hulman, Tony 75
Hulme, Denis 229
Hundt, 159
Hunt, Reg 227–228
Huntoon, George 128
Hutton, Barbara 219
HWM 18, 48, 112, 128–129
HWM-Jaguar *65*
Hyde Park Hotel 41–42

Iglesias, Jesus 33
Indianapolis Speedway 21,
*75,* 94–102, 198
Indianapolis 500-Mile Race
21, 92, 173
1952 94
1953 94, 96
1954 94
1955 *75,* 94–102
1960 96
1961 229
International Six Days Trial
196
Invicta 129
Ireland, Innes 113
Isle of Man 206
Issigonis, Alex 25
Italian Automobile Club 121

253

Italian GP
  1924 117
  1954 96
  1955 *182, 185,* 198

Jackson-Moore, Roy 130–131
Jacobs, Dick 126
Jaguar 25, *76, 78,* 109, 132,
  134, 141, 145–146, 153,
  162, 196, 206–207, 214,
  231, 247
  C-type 26
  D-type 25, *78–79,* 126, 130,
    138–140, 144, *187,*
    194–195, 207–208,
    212–213, 231
  XK120 30, 196
  2.4-litre saloon 24
  3.4/3.8-litre saloons 24
Jano, Vittorio 116–118,
  122–123
JAP engines 173
Jarrott, Charles 135
Jeep 100
Jenkinson, Denis 46–57, *68,*
  *70–71,* 81–82, 195, 197,
  242
Jim Robbins Special 98
Johnson, 144
Johnston, Sherwood 25
Jones, Alan 31, 227
Jones, Stan 31, 227–228
Jopp, Peter 208–209

Karlskoga 196
Keck, Howard 97
Keegan, Rupert 23
Keen, Mike 227
Keller, 98, 99
Kelly, Grace 218
Kentucky Fried Chicken 23
Keser, Artur 159, 174, 230
Klemantaski, Louis 53, 113
Kling, Karl 33, 35–36, 48–49,
  52, 54–55, 112, 114–115,
  142, 144, 146–148, 156,
  161, 165, 168–170, 174,
  *179, 181–182, 185, 187,*
  196, 200–201, 207, 230,
  235, 247
  comments on Le Mans
    tragedy 147–148
Könecke, Dr Fritz 154, 164
Kosteletzky, 167
Kretschmann, 211
Kristianstadt circuit *182,* 194,
  196
Kroc, Ray 23

Lago, Anthony 136, 138
Lago Talbot 228
Lamm, 167
Lampredi, Aurelio 59

Lancia 33–35, 37, 64, 82–88,
  90, 92, 111–123, 128,
  171, 200
  D24 118
  D50 22, 34, 36, *73–74,* 92,
    111–123, 171, 199, 205
Lancia, Gianni 118–120, 122
Lancia, Vincenzo 117
Lancia-Ferrari 122
Lang, Herrmann 195
Lappen circuit 196
Le Mans 24-Hour Race 247
  1935 28
  1937 28
  1939 29
  1949 125
  1950 125
  1951 124–125
  1952 *80,* 135–136, 160
  1953 26, 162
  1954 43, 162
  1955 *77–80,* 115, 160, 217,
    238
    disaster 21–22, *78,*
      126–127, 132–159, 168,
      *177, 179,* 211, 245
  1959 115
Le Mans starts 208–209
Lelong, Jacques 133
Leston, Les 237–243
Levegh (Velghe), Pierre *80,*
  135–136
Levegh, Pierre *78, 80,* 126,
  133–138, 142–157, *177,*
  245
Linch, John 239
Little Madonie circuit 231
Lloyd, 128
Lockett, Johnny 77, 126–127,
  208
Loens, André 196
Lord, Leonard 127
Lotus 96, 160, 163, 209, 211,
  238
  Type 49 117
Lotus-Climax 208
Lotus-Connaught 43
Lotus Cortina 200
Lotus-MG 44, 208
Lund, Ted 77, 126–127
Lurani, Count Giovanni
  (Johnny) 45, 88, 91

Macklin, Lance 18, 53, 64,
  *78,* 128, 130, 133–134,
  140, 142–144, 147–149,
  152–153, *177,* 208, 211
Macklin, Sir Noel 129
Maggi, Count Aymo 45, 139
Maglioli, Umberto 33, 36–38,
  53, 55, 89, 118, 140, 200,
  231
Mahl Pistons 249

Mainwaring, Richard 213
Mantovani, Sergio 33, 35
Manzon, Robert 231, 235, 241
Marchand, René 136
Margaret, Princess 23
Marimón, Onofre 243
Marr, Leslie 173, 193
  GP memories 176, 193
Marzotto, Paolo 53
Maserati 12, 34–36, 64,
  81–82, 92, 114, 119–120,
  130, 145, 169, 175, *187,*
  194, 200, 206, 208, 213,
  231, 237–238, 241–243
Maserati models 25
  A6GC 91
  A6GCM 30
  4CL 30
  4CLT 91
  4CLT/48 30–31, 91
  8CM 28
  250F 22, 30–32, 35, 38, 61,
    64, *65,* 85, 112, 129, 166,
    169, 171, 173, 200,
    226–228, 243
Matra 170
Maybach Special 31, 227
Mayers, Jim 208–211, 213
Mays, Raymond 28, 41
Mazzotti, Count Franco 45
McAlpine, Ken 140, 144
McDonald's 23
McGrath, Jack 98
McHenry, Troy 222
McLaren, Bruce 32, 96
McLaren, Les 32
McLaren-Offenhauser M16
  96
Melbourne Olympic Games
  32
Mediteguy, Carlos 33, 35
Mercedes-Benz 34–36, 46,
  48, 54–59, 63–64, *71–73,*
  *78, 80,* 81, 83–84, 93, 96,
  106, 116, 119–120,
  133–134, 137, 140–142,
  144, 146, 156, 164,
  169–171, 174–175, *179,*
  *186–187,* 195, 197–200,
  202, 206–212, 219,
  230–231, 235, 245, 249
  air brakes *79–80,* 160–163,
    *178, 181, 189,* 199
  withdrawal from
    motorsport 22, *78,* 158,
    170, *190,* 197, 230
Mercedes-Benz models
  W125 64
  W154 247, 250
  W196 18, 22, 33–34, 48, 63,
    *66, 74–75,* 77, 92, 112,
    114–115, 170–171, *180,*
    *185,* 195, 202, 247

220 49, 52
220A 57
300SL 25, 132, 195–196, 209, 219, 231, 247
300SLR 19, 21, 34, 37, 46–57, *68–70, 80*, 145, 160, *177–178, 182, 190–191*, 194, 212, 214, 231, 235, 245, 249
300SLR GT Coupé *192*, 197–198, 207, 245–248
Simplex 248
Mercedes museum 247
Merrick, Tony 247–250
Meyer, Lou 94
MG 43, 77, 124–125, 208
  K3 125
  Magnette 27
  MGA 77, 124–126
  TC 125
  TD 125
  TF 125, 216
  XPAG engine 125
Mières, Roberto 33, 36, 64, 83, 112, 114, 166, 172, 200
Miles, Ken 126, 216
Mille Miglia
  1930 201
  1940 90
  1953 217
  1954 92, 118, 217
  1955 11, 45–58, *68–71*, 84, 112, 130, 139, 195, 197, 217, 231
Miller, Peter 209, 213–214
Minozzi, Giovanni 90
Minter Field 216
Modena circuit 91
Mölter, Gunther 230
Monaco 28, 173, 205
Monaco GP 22, 59, 64
  1952 64
  1955 62–64, *71–76*, 82–83, 93, 103, 112–113, 119, 121, 129, 168, 170
  1956 122
  1958 *72*, 86
  1967 *76*
Monte Carlo 203–204
Montlhéry circuit 82, 84
Monza 74, 111, 116–117, 122, *182, 185*, 198–205, 246
  banked track *182*, 198
  1,000km race 88
Morley, Bryan 60
Morris
  B-series engine 126
  B-series twin-cam engine 127
  Minor 25
Morris, Peter 227

Mors 135–136
Moss, Alfred 211–212
Moss, Stirling 18, 33, 35–36, 38, 42–43, 46–57, 59, 63, *66, 68–71, 73, 75–76, 78*, 83–85, 92, 104, 105, 107, 112, 114, 120, 128–129, 144–145, 156, 161–162, 165, 167–168, 173, *178–182, 185–186, 189–191*, 194–197, 201, 207–208, 211, 213–214, 231–235
  diaries 81, 86–87, 172
  driving style 199–200
  first GP win 11, 26, 174–175
  lap records/fastest laps 174, 185, 195, 211–212, 235
  Mercedes sports car world title 46
  Mille Miglia win 19, 21
  pole positions 169, 172, *181*
  race wins 11, 26, 46–47, 51, *71*, 84, 169, *180–181*
  signing to Mercedes team 22, 38, *190*, 235
*Motor, The* magazine 246
*Motor Sport* magazine 12, 48, 50, 55, 172, 197, 242
*Motor Yearbook 1956, The* 21
Mundy, Harry 160, 162
Musso, Luigi 33, 64, 112, 145, 166, 200, 208, 231, 241–243
Musy, Benoit 194, 208

Nabakov, Vladimir 23
Nallinger, Dr Fritz 159, 164–165
Napier, John 206
Naples GP 1955 92, 119
Neal, 228
Neubauer, Alfred 18, 36, 38, 54, *66*, 71, 81, 106, 143–144, 146, 159, 165, 167, 174, *181*, 195, 201, 212, 230, 232
Le Mans tragedy report 146–153
Neufeld, Dr 222
New Zealand GP
  1954 227
  1955 27, 31, *65*
New Zealand Motor Cup *65*
Nixon, Chris 81, 84, 245
Northcy, Percy 206
Nürburgring 111, 116, 138, 168, 195, 219, 245–246
Nuvoari, Tazio 47, *77*, 116, 126, 199
Nye, Doug 56, 226

Offenhauser engines 92, 97, 144
Oldsmobile V8 engines 96
Oliver, Eric 48
Oliver, Mike 237, 239, 242
Orange circuit 227
OSCA 128
  V12 engine 30–31
OSCA-Maserati 30–31
Owen Organisation 171

Palm Springs 216
Paris Motor Show 24
Paris-Toulouse-Paris race 135
Parkes, J. J. 25
Parkes, Michael 25
Parnell, Reg 208, 237
Pedralbes circuit 92
Perdisa, Cesare 83, 85, 112
Phillips, George 124
Pierrepoint, Albert 39
Piotti, Luigi 241
Pirelli tyres 122
Pollet, Jacques 64, 241
Pomona Fairgrounds 222
Pomeroy, Laurence 246
Poore, Dennis 208
Porsche 22, 51, 127, 145, 195, 208, 211, 217
  356 1500 Speedster *189*, 216, 219
  550RS 1500 Spyder 23, *189*, 215, 217, 219, 221–223
Porsche, Ferdinand 231
Port Wakefield circuit 225, 227–228
Presley, Elvis 57
Prost, Alain 23
Purdue University Band 94
Purdy, Ken 50–51, 199

*Racers* film 81–82
Railton 129
Railton, Reid 125
Raymond, Robert 129
*Rebel Without a Cause* film 22, *189*, 215
Reims circuit 22, 31, 43, 59, 84, 91, 115, 170, 217
Repco V8 engine 229
Reuters 132–134
Reventlow, Lance 219
Richardson, Miranda 40
Riley
  Imp 27, *65*
  engines 41
Ripon, Alan 125
Riverside Records 103, 105, 109–110
Road America race 25
*Road & Track* magazine 113
Roebuck, Nigel 49, 103–105, 109, 172, 204

Rolls-Royce 206
  Silver Cloud 24
Rolt, Tony 193
Rootes 24
Rose, Mauri 94
Rosier, Louis 241
Russell, Jim 211
Royal Automobile Club 168, 172
Rubirosa, 128
Rutherford, Douglas 83, 85
Ruttman, Troy 98

Salinas circuit 23, 218–219
Salk, Jonas 23
Salvadori, Roy 32, 173, 194–195, 208, 237, 241–242
Samuelson, Dickie 239
San Remo circuit 91
San Sebastian GP 1924 21, 192, 236
Santa Barbara 216
Sanders, Harland 23
Sanesi, Consalvo 91
Scarab 219
Schell, Harry 33, 35–36, 63, 172–174, 185, 200, 241–243
Schumacher, Michael 59, 107
Scuderia Ambrosiana 91
Seaman, Richard 219
  memorial stone 114
Sebring circuit 128–129, 231
  12-hour race 128
Segrave, Henry 11, 21, 192, 236
Setright, L. J. K. 60, 175
Shaw, Wilbur 94
Shelby, Carroll 105, 130, 208, 241, 243
Shell 237
Sighinolfi, 231
Silverstone circuit 30, 32, 91, 169, 231
Daily Express International Trophy 30
Simon, André 64, 81, 83, 144, 156, 172–173, 207, 214
Singer Motors 24
  engine 43
Smith, Bill 208–210
Snetterton circuit 226
Sommer, Raymond 29
Spa-Francorchamps 59, 77, 111–113, 120, 170, 203
Spanish GP
  1954 92, 119
  1955 cancelled 166
Sports Car Club of America 216
SS 196

Steering Wheel Club 42–43
Steinbeck, John 218
Stewart, Jackie 138, 145
Stewart, Jimmy 138–139, 145
Stirling Moss Ltd 129
Stoop, Dickie 127
Straight, Whitney 28
Strieff, Philippe 23
Studebaker 100
Suzuki, Toshio 23
Swaters, Jacques 139, 187, 208
Swedish GP 1955 46, 182, 194–197
Sweikert, Bob 75, 100, 102
Swiss GP
  1953 92
  1954 96
  1955 cancelled 166
Syracuse GP 11, 19, 21, 192, 236–237, 240–241

Talbot 80, 135–138, 173
Tanner, Hans 60
Targa Florio
  1924 231
  1953 118
  1954 118
  1955 46, 190–191, 230–235
Taruffi, Piero 53, 55, 63, 91, 113, 118, 168–170, 174, 179, 181–182, 185, 200–202, 231
Thompson, Eric 140, 144
Titterington, Desmond 191, 207, 212–213, 230, 234–235, 237
Tourist Trophy
  1905 206
  1932 126
  1955 46, 127, 186, 189, 206–214, 231, 238, 247
Townsend, Peter 23
Traco Engineering 96
Travers, Jim 96
Trenberth, 228
Trintignant, Louis 86
Trintignant, Maurice 37–38, 63–64, 72, 83–86, 112, 121, 200
Triumph TR2/TR3 25
Turin GP 1955 92, 119
Turnupseed, Donald 215, 221, 223
Tyrrell 61
Tyrrell, Ken 196

Uhlenhaut, Rudi 71, 159, 166–167, 181, 192, 197–198, 202, 204, 245–248
Ulster Trophy 208

Ustinov, Sir Peter 13, 76, 103–110

Valentario, 241
Valenzano, 145
Vandervell, G. A. 112, 173
Vanwall 107, 112, 172–173, 175, 185, 200–201, 226
Vauxhall
  T 41
  30/98 41
Vauxhall-Villiers 41
Villiers, Amherst 41
Villoresi, Luigi 33, 35, 64, 91–92, 96, 118–119, 169, 199–200, 231, 241–243
Volkswagen 43
  Beetle 24
von Delius, Carl 219
von Delius, Ernst 219
von Korff, 150, 152
von Neumann, Johnny 217, 219, 221
von Trips, Wolfgang 104, 195–196, 207, 212, 214, 247
Vukovich, Bill 21, 75, 94–102

Waeffler, Hans 126
Walker, Murray 63
Walker, Rob 25–26, 72, 86, 208
Ward, Roger 98–99, 101
Water Speed Record 24
Weslake, Harry 127–128
Wharton, Ken 173, 185, 210–211
Wheeler, RA, Charles 27
Wheels magazine 228
Whicker, Alan 76
White Mouse Stable 28
Whiteford, Doug 228
Whitehead, Peter 31–32
Whitmore, James 217–218
Wilkins, Gordon 246
Wilkins, Joe 239–240
Williams GP team 31, 194, 204
Wimille, Jean-Pierre 86, 91
Winterbottom, Eric 125
Wood, Natalie 224
World Sports Car Championship 189, 206, 230–231, 235
Wuetherich, Rolf 217–222
Wyer, John 196, 238

Yedor, Cy 216
Young, Eoin 49
Young, John 208

Zandvoort circuit 30, 43, 164–166, 178–179, 200